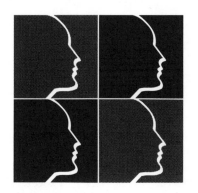

People Smarts

Bending the Golden Rule to Give Others What They Want

Tony Alessandra, Ph.D.
and Michael J. O'Connor, Ph.D.

With
Janice Van Dyke

Pfeiffer
& COMPANY

Amsterdam • Johannesburg • Oxford
San Diego • Sydney •Toronto

Published by Pfeiffer & Company
8517 Production Avenue
San Diego, CA 92121-2280

This publication is designed to provide accurate and authoritative information in regard to the subject matter covered. It is sold with the understanding that the publisher is not engaged in rendering legal, accounting, or other professional service. If legal advice or other expert assistance is required, the services of a competent professional person should be sought. *From a Declaration of Principles jointly adopted by a Committee of the American Bar Association and a Committee of Publishers.*

Editor: Marian Prokop
Interior Design and Page Composition: Judy Whalen
Cover: John Odam Design Associates

Library of Congress Cataloging-in-Publication Data

Alessandra, Anthony J.
    People smarts : bending the golden rule to give others what they want / Tony Alessandra and Michael J. O'Connor.
        p.   cm.
    Includes index.
    ISBN 0-88390-421-7
    1. Interpersonal relations.   I. O'Connor, Michael J., 1944-
II. Title.
HM132.A3545   1994
158.2—dc20   94-8602
                                                          CIP

Printed in the United States of America.
Printing 1 2 3 4 5 6 7 8 9 10

Dedications

From Tony:

I dedicate this book to Jim Cathcart, a fellow professional speaker and my closest friend. Over the years, Jim has helped me to grow professionally as a keynote speaker and author and has always been there for me with open ears, an open mind, and relevant advice. His unselfish friendship has made my life a much richer and happier one.

From Michael:

- To Mary Ann, my loving wife and my greatest teacher

- To my children, Kevin and Kara, for their continuing patience, tolerance, and appreciation of my life's work

- And to my colleagues and clients for sharing their experiences and feedback

Table of Contents

Acknowledgments

Writing this book has become more and more a team effort as we have progressed from one state to the next. Some people contributed content, either directly or indirectly; others also gave helpful comments about the manuscript; some recharged our batteries when the going got rough; and some reached seemingly unreachable deadlines to keep the project going on time.

With this in mind, the authors would like to thank Jim Cathcart, John Geier, Carl Jung, William Marston, David McClelland, David Merrill, Isabel Briggs Myers, Katherine Briggs, and Larry Wilson for their pioneering research and writings.

Those who gave valuable feedback on the manuscript include Rick Barrera, Sheila Murray-Bethel, Charles Boyd, Don Cipriano, Marcia Feener, Jay Lewis, and Judy Zitloff.

Many others contributed input on their own particular personality types—Linda Acker, Sue Alessandra, Colleen Alessandra, Gary Alessandra, Jessica and Justin Alessandra, Margaret Alessandra, Dr. Jeff Applestein, Bill Arens, Gregg Baron, Lynn Cablk, Catherine Carpenter, Dave Catchpole, Holli Catchpole, Paula Cathcart, Danny Colleran, Jeff Davidson, Ron Friedman, Victor Geberin, Warren Greshes, Scott Higby, Phil Hunsaker, Jo Hunsaker, Sam Kephart, John Lee, Stan and Melody Leopard, Dr. Seymour Myers, Mikala Rahn, Maryfaith Schweighardt, Hal Small, and Pete Wheeler.

Preface

Getting along with others is the universal key to success. Studies have shown that all highly successful people share the ability to build rapport with others. With this book, you hold the key to successful associations in every area of your life. With the strategies we're about to show you, you can build rapport even with strangers and get your way with everyone.

We'll share with you techniques developed over more than three decades of working with and for people whose success depended on their relationship with others. That description might really apply to all of us; we all, to some degree, can benefit from positive relationships with others to get what we need or want.

You'll discover how to be better liked, be a better communicator, and reduce tension and conflict in all your encounters. With the innovative, step-by-step techniques in this book, you'll be able to see yourself as you never have before—through the eyes of others. You'll learn how to create the impression that makes an impact on all kinds of people—the impact that helps people succeed and achieve.

This book has three purposes: (1) to give you a conscious awareness of what people do, (2) to help you predict what people are likely to do and why they do it, and (3) to help you accept yourself and others as worthwhile so you can adapt and successfully relate to them.

Our behavioral style model is simple, practical, easy to remember and use, and extremely accurate. You'll recognize the differences in people and use those differences to make almost any situation work for you. And the differences we see on the outside are real clues to what is going on inside someone's head.

People Smarts will help you connect with people and succeed in the ways most of us want to succeed, but don't know how to accomplish. In this book, you'll read the step-by-step outline of just how and why these relationship strategies can work for you.

These specific lessons will give you three major keys to success:

1. How to understand your own style, its strengths and weaknesses, and how you communicate and interact with others.

2. How to identify someone else's style so you can treat them the way they need and want to be treated.

3. How to adapt your style so that you make all kinds of people more at ease with you and you more at ease with them. When people are comfortable, they'll want to do business with you, spend time with you, and seek you out to share good things with you.

This book gives you the tools to get what you want in various life situations. It equips you with the power and knowledge to cash in on these insights through more positive and productive exchanges with others. You can now more realistically take charge of improving your relationships—because this book shows you how.

A.J.A. and M.J.O.

Introduction

People everywhere want to find out more about themselves and about how to deal with others more effectively. This book shows you a simple, yet proven, way to influence others positively.

You will learn to see people as they really are and to get the most out of relationships with others. This book does not deal with values or judgments. Instead, it concentrates on needs and fears—our natural tendencies that cause us to do the things we do.

In this book, you will learn specific strategies for dealing successfully with all kinds of people, even the most difficult ones. You will learn how to read someone's behavioral style over the phone or through a letter; you will also find tips for how to prepare for meetings with each type of person.

The material in this book was developed over three decades of work with hundreds of thousands of people in all walks of life. We have proven its validity by putting into action what you will learn—how to manage any interpersonal situation to your ultimate gain and the gain of others.

Behavioral Style

In dealing with people, you have developed a certain style with which you are comfortable. When you communicate with others, you may be clear about what you want to say,

1

but the message that is received is affected in two ways: (1) by your style of delivery, and (2) by the recipient's background and how he or she processes the message and interaction.

Every person has his or her own special way of doing things, as well as an identifiable and predictable behavioral type. Behavioral type is a pattern, a group of recurring habits, centering on how you deal with people and situations. It is your comfortable method of behaving, most of the time, when you relax and just act yourself.

For example, one type of person measures success by results. He heads for the finished product and the bottom line. He'll do whatever it takes, within reason, to get the job done. In fact, his natural response to what he views as other people's lack of accomplishment is, "Don't just sit around wasting time! Get busy!" He needs achievements.

Another type places high value on recognition and measures success by the amount of acknowledgment and praise she receives. Consequently, she typically follows that route to attention and applause. She gravitates toward friendliness and enjoyment, popularity and prestige—while consciously avoiding rejection, negativism, and arguments.

Then we have the steady, cooperative type of person who needs close relationships. He places a high value on sharing and trust, but bases his feelings about people and things on concrete evidence. He wants the security and predictability found in daily routine, so he resists sudden, unplanned changes and needs stable, predictable environments. This person thrives on the familiar. Changes or surprises make him uncomfortable.

The last type concerns herself more with content than with congratulations. She wants to know how things work so she can evaluate how correctly they function. Because she needs to be right, she prefers checking processes herself. Concerned with appearances, she focuses on the process—how to perform a task—while complying with established rules and regulations. Tasks win over people and a slow pace prevails.

We have labeled these four behavior styles as the Director, the Socializer, the Relater, and the Thinker. We will talk about behavioral style throughout the rest of the book, particularly how it helps and hinders relationships.

Modifying Your Style

Your interactions with people succeed when you receive and heed their external signals; they fail when you ignore and cross these signals. When you understand something about your own habitual style and how it differs from other people's styles, you can modify your approach to get on the same wavelength with them. The ideas that you present to them do not change. But you can change the way you present those ideas. And people will teach you how to treat them if you are willing to discover their unique signals.

Often, when we do what comes naturally we alienate others without realizing it. That same behavior may not be natural for them. If we want to get along with our colleagues, employees, bosses, friends, and families, it is essential that we become aware of our natural tendencies—and their natural preferences! Then we can defuse extreme behaviors before we sabotage ourselves. We do this by temporarily using behavior modification to change our own behavior so that the other person feels comfortable. When this happens, tension lessens and co-operation zooms.

These strategies can pay off for every one of us—in better business associations and hence, better business. They can help us to improve our relationships with our coworkers by handling the unpleasant but inevitable friction we all encounter at times. You will learn to minimize annoying behaviors in others and how to spot and reduce these same behaviors in yourself. You will learn more about others and about how others see you.

Bottom-Line Results

This book will not only help you become a better you, it also will help you behave more maturely and produc-tively. It will teach you how to focus on your goals instead of your fears. Then you can develop and use more of your natural strengths, while recognizing, improving on, and developing your less developed areas. We do not make judgments in this book about which behaviors are good or bad. Instead, we'll concentrate on our individual needs and fears—our natural tendencies that cause us to do what we do—and on how we can deal with these to help ourselves and others to be more effective.

Managers need to know how to maximize their staff members' productivity and efficiency; salespeople seek to build better rapport with customers; and employees want to get along with their peers and managers. Those in helping professions want to provide better care for their patients and clients. Engineers want to fit into their workplace as they turn out more quality products. Diplomats and public officials desire to influence varying groups so they can improve communication—whether internationally, nationally, or locally. In short, virtually everyone has a stake in making their working relationships better.

This is a reader-friendly book, with lots of charts and graphs to summarize and explain the text. You will use and reuse it as a constant companion for dealing with difficult people and stressful situations. You will begin to understand both your own unique strengths and inherent shortcomings and those of others. And you will learn the tools you need to take charge of improving all of your work relationships.

1

Bending the
Golden Rule

Personality Clash or Instant Rapport?

In your dealings with others, have you ever experienced a personality conflict? No matter how hard you may try, you clench your teeth, and your body pumps more adrenalin whenever you are with this difficult character. Whatever you may want to call the process, you clash. The two of you are just not tuned in on the same wavelength.

When two people clash, they often move toward extremes: Either they avoid each other or they tell each other exactly what they think about such unacceptable behavior. Or they may tell everyone else how distasteful they find each other. Or they may just grit their teeth and tolerate the situation. Whatever the initial reaction, these two people feel uncomfortable because they are experiencing a personality conflict.

On the other hand, you certainly can think of somebody you liked immediately. The two of you had instant rapport, immediate chemistry. After ten minutes you felt as if you'd known Mr. or Ms. Wonderful for half a lifetime. Here was a soul mate who connected with you from the start. His or her personality "felt right," and you also felt good about yourself when the two of you were together. You were relaxed and comfortable with this person. Chemistry prevailed, and he or she made your list of favorite people.

What could possibly account for these two extreme variations in the human species? Certainly unique sets of experiences, coupled with the genes passed down through the family, ensure that all people are different. Everyone's ideas vary about the kinds of people to avoid and the kinds of people who make best friends. Given these subjective differences, how people communicate can result in conflict or chemistry. So how do you go about interacting with all of those diverse, sometimes difficult, people out there?

How to Deal With Difficult People

The ideas in this book will teach you how to treat people in a way that allows them to feel comfortable with you. As a result, there will be less tension between you two. When tension goes down, positive outcomes—trust, credibility, creativity, cooperation, respect, commitment, and productivity—go up. How do you get results with people? By communicating with them on their level so they feel at ease. Because challenging relationships are realities, we'd like to show you how to

- Understand your own style, its strengths and weaknesses, and how your behaviors communicate that style to others

- Identify the styles of others by quick, easily learned techniques so you will know how to "read people" and treat them the way they would like to be treated

- Adjust your behavior to make all kinds of people more at ease with you and you with them

Practicing the Golden Rule

You can create much more chemistry and far less conflict in all your relationships—work, social, dating, and family—based on how well you practice the Golden Rule. If you exercise the Golden Rule appropriately, you can create much more relationship chemistry. But if you fail to understand the true spirit of the Golden Rule, you will create many more personality conflicts. To make sure you have the proper perspective, what is the Golden Rule?

By the Golden Rule, we mean simply, "Do unto others as you would have them do unto you." Not the managerial version—"The person with the gold makes the rules,"—or the skeptical interpretation—"Do unto others *before* they do unto you."

The Golden Rule

Do unto others as you would have
them do unto you.

"So," you say, "how could people get in trouble if they practiced that truth? Living by the Golden Rule should result in more harmonious relationships, not create conflict!" You're right. The problem lies with practicing the Golden Rule verbatim and not understanding its true intent. When you misapply the Golden Rule, you stand a much greater chance of triggering conflict than you do of fostering chemistry.

The explanation is simple. When you treat others as you want to be treated, you can end up offending others who have different needs, wants, and expectations than you do. Therefore, when you apply the Golden Rule verbatim, you have a much greater chance of triggering conflict than you do chemistry. Yes, you heard that statement correctly. If you apply the Golden Rule literally, you will have problems with up to 75 percent of the people you meet. Following the Golden Rule verbatim means treating others from your own point of view; it means speaking in the way you are most comfortable listening; it means selling to others the way you like to be sold; and it means managing the way you want others to direct you.

When you treat people as you seek to be treated, it can cause tension because the other person may not like your way. You may act to fill your own needs or speak in a way that seems easy for you to follow. However, these behaviors may not meet the needs of the other person. This is the second reason that the Golden Rule actually can damage relationships: It implies that all people want to be treated in the same way, when, in fact, our preferences are not alike. So application of this principle varies from one individual to the next based on their personality differences.

Example: Margaret

The Golden Rule would work in a world in which all of us were identical, but we are not identical. For instance, Tony's mother, Margaret, devoutly practices it, only to have it backfire. She treats everybody alike, as if the world population were part of her extended Italian family. Margaret is an exceptionally people-oriented, outgoing person. When she goes to a restaurant, she greets the host and other patrons as though they were in her kitchen; anyone who makes eye contact with her is fair game.

As she approaches a table of complete strangers, she typically says, "Hello! My name is Margaret. What's yours? Are you Italian? No? Too bad...." And on and on. She joins in other people's conversations. Because she doesn't mind being asked personal questions, she asks other people personal questions—whether they want to answer or not.

> *Margaret:* "What do you do for a living?"
>
> *Patron:* "I'm an actuary."
>
> *Margaret:* "An actuary. Is that a religious society or something? And what do you do as an actuary?"
>
> *Patron:* "I calculate rates for insurance companies."
>
> *Margaret:* "Do you make good money? Yes? How much?"

If we take a poll at that restaurant, half the people will probably think that Margaret Alessandra is wonderful. ("Boy, I wish my mother acted like that," or, "The woman is a national treasure.") The rest of them are likely to react or think differently. ("I enjoy my privacy when I go out to eat," or even, "Who let her loose?") As well-meaning and people oriented as she is, she often steps on people's toes unintentionally.

What has happened? Margaret puts the Golden Rule into action; by doing so, she impresses some people and depresses others. Well, maybe she doesn't exactly depress them, but she certainly heightens their tensions. By acting the way she likes to be treated, she gets mixed reviews. By behaving from only her own perspective, she is not taking others' preferences into account. Why not? Simply because she doesn't mind if strangers approach her and ask about her intimate, private thoughts, she naturally assumes it's okay for her to do the same thing. This is true for the rest of us. If we don't think first of the other person, we run the risk of unintentionally imposing a tension-filled "win/lose" or "lose/lose" relationship on them.

The Spirit of the Golden Rule

We believe in bending the Golden Rule to consider the feelings of the other person. Notice that we are not saying that you should break the rule. Instead we redefine it to be "Do unto others as they want to be done unto," or "Treat others as they wish to be treated." This bending of the Golden Rule does not imply "better." It simply captures the true spirit or actual intention of the Golden Rule and leads us to consider and respond appropriately to the other person's needs. We can learn to treat different people differently, according to their needs, not ours; this will lead to greater understanding and acceptance.

The Spirit of the Golden Rule

Do unto others as they would have
you do unto them,

or

Treat others as they wish to be treated.

Doing What Comes Naturally

When we treat another person from our own perspective, the result is often tension, whether it is expressed or not. In Neil Simon's play *The Odd Couple,* Felix Unger and Oscar Madison represent opposite types. Oscar perceives himself as a "real" man—rough and tumble; Felix views Oscar as a slob. Felix sees himself as a "model of perfection"; Oscar figures Felix is an uptight worrywart. Whenever Felix approaches Oscar with his own expectations based on his own needs—tidiness, punctuality, and moderation—Oscar explodes. Although the two characters exaggerate many behaviors that people encounter, they represent clear examples of how we can turn people off when we "act naturally." Although watching Felix and Oscar clash may be entertaining, it's not so much fun in the daily lives of the real Felixes and Oscars around the world.

A steady dose of conflicting needs can end a promising relationship unless we treat the other person appropriately. If Felix and Oscar made the effort to understand each other's needs, they could begin to gain greater appreciation of and learn more about their differences. Then they could find practical options for solving their own "naturally occurring" conflicts. The two of them collide when one expects the other to act like his clone.

Every day we face the potential for conflict or success with different types of people. Conflicts are inevitable, but the outcomes from how you handle dissension are more controllable. At the very least, you can manage your end of it. You can choose to treat somebody from his or her own perspective, the way that person wants to be treated, by modifying your own behavior; or you can choose to meet only your own needs—facing consequences such as dissatisfaction, frustration, confusion, and distress. It's up to you.

Modify Your Spots

"Modify my behavior? I don't want to change! And I hate phonies!"

We're not talking about changing a leopard into an elephant. We mean acting in a sensible, successful way. When someone wants to move at a faster pace, move at that pace. If other people want more facts and details, provide them.

"But wait; isn't it phony to act in a way that isn't natural for me?"

Actually, we think that people are likely to appreciate and accept us more when we act in ways that are responsive to our environment. The result is greater success! Such behavior helps to dispel the "Ugly American" stereotype that has been associated with some tourists who "act naturally" and expect the natives to act like they do. Of course, anything that is new feels strange at first, until you get more comfortable with it through repeated practice.

People learn to become more adaptable through education, experience, and maturity. We simply have to allow the opportunity for appropriate behaviors to surface. As we've mentioned, if you're able to put yourself in the other person's position, you become more open-minded in dealing with him or her. When you understand the way the other person feels comfortable communicating, you can modify your approach. This does not mean that you have changed your own natural personality. You merely have added on more consciously learned, behavioral insights and strengths for dealing with different types of people and situations. People will teach you how to communicate with them if you are willing to learn their signals by "reading" and then responding to them appropriately.

A Suggestion for Felix and Oscar

Felix Unger and Oscar Madison, the "Odd Couple," have known each other for years. But they don't always choose to apply what they know about each other. When each considers only himself, he unconsciously plunges ahead toward meeting only his own needs. By doing this, he ignores the signals of how to meet the other person's needs as well.

Imagine this more productive exchange:

Felix: "Oscar, your room is a mess. Here, I'll help you straighten it up by throwing away these old newspapers."

Oscar: "Okay, but don't touch anything else in my room without my approval, Felix. You'll ruin my personal filing system."

Oscar's housekeeping is intentionally looser than Felix prefers it to be. If Felix can tolerate a more "lived in" look and if Oscar can learn to pick up after himself, they'll become more successful at meeting each other's needs. Regarding the housekeeping issue, Felix needs orderliness, and Oscar needs freedom. With this realization in mind, they can communicate more effectively by letting each other know they have received these two signals. Then they can explore ways for satisfying both types of needs.

One option is trading off. Oscar can keep his room as sloppy as he wants as long as the door is closed, and their common living area is neat. Or they can collaborate by cleaning Oscar's room together.

> *Felix:* "Oscar, I know you like your freedom to do what you want, but your room is so filled with personal expressions you seem to be a prisoner in it. [How does he find his bed?] I'd like to help you organize your room so that it's more comfortable for you and for me."
>
> *Oscar:* [Ha! Felix would probably throw everything out if it was his room.] "I like it the way it is, but I'll go along with your idea if you don't throw anything away without asking me first."

Felix and Oscar have reached a naturally agreeable solution based on understanding and accepting each other's needs. Good for them!

Background of Behavioral Types

People have been both frustrated and fascinated with one another's differences for thousands of years. The earliest recorded efforts were made by astrologers who recorded the positions of the heavens. The twelve signs of the zodiac in four basic groupings—Earth, Air, Fire, and Water—are still used today.

In ancient Greece, Hippocrates' concept of four temperaments followed—Sanguine, Phlegmatic, Melancholic, and Choleric. He viewed personality as shaped by blood, phlegm, black bile, and yellow bile. As unpalatable as this might sound to us, people accepted these physical or bodily causes for varying "humours" for centuries. Respected figures from medical/physical sciences, metaphysics, mathematics, and philosophy observed these four temperaments—including Aristotle, Empedocles, Theophrastus, and, in Roman times, Galen. References to Hippocrates' four temperaments can be found in Shakespeare's plays. We still use these terms, especially concerning babies and young children. "Jason looks so serious and melancholy for a child," or "Jennifer has a sanguine, ruddy-faced disposition."

In 1921, Dr. Carl Gustav Jung wrote *Psychological Types*, at that time the most sophisticated scientific work on personality. Primarily it explains that people do not all have the same basic orientations or ways of perceiving, interpreting, and responding to the world. Jung described four basic behavioral styles—Intuitor, Thinker, Feeler, and Sensor.

This basic, four-type model spans all cultures, East and West, north and south. Most of the explanations of behavioral styles focus on internal characteristics leading to external behaviors. Our concept focuses on the patterns of observable, external behaviors that each style shows to the rest of the world. It also demystifies those lesser known, but scientifically proven, internal forces that are the motivating clues behind people's behaviors. In other words, this book will help you to understand why people do what they do. Because we can see and hear external behaviors, we can read other people.

Our model is simple, practical, easy to remember and use, and extremely accurate. It divides people into four natural, core behavioral types:

- The Director
- The Socializer
- The Relater
- The Thinker

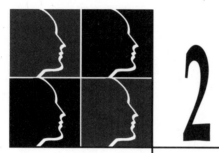

2

I Know Who You Are, but What Am I?

Your Behavioral Type

How do you identify your behavioral type? You begin by choosing those traits that most and least describe you from a list of one-word possibilities. At first, you might think, "All of these words sound like me," or "None of them sound like me"; but select your personal traits from these commonly found choices with a clear focus in mind. Your reward will be in arriving at one behavioral type that is more descriptive of you than any of the others.

All people occasionally behave like another type, but we behave in predominantly one style most of the time. The most familiar style, the one in which you operate most comfortably, is your core behavioral type—your own unique personality style, which is most evident when you just "act yourself." To discover your behavioral type, read the instructions carefully and answer accordingly.

The Personal Assets Inventory

The Personal Assets Inventory is a realistic measure of your actual behaviors. Think of your personal traits across the variety of environments and periods in your life, and complete the inventory as you see yourself. This inventory can be a valuable personal resource for identifying (1) your already developed personal characteristics and (2) other potential strengths you can further develop. You can learn to adapt your style to handle different types of situations, even the more "difficult" ones that we encounter in the real-world laboratory of life.

23

Instructions for Responding and Scoring

1. In the space provided below, identify those behaviors in terms of how characteristic of you they are. In each row, assign 4 points to the behavior that is most characteristic of you; assign 3 points to the next most characteristic behavior, then 2, and finally 1 point to the behavior that is least characteristic of you.

Example

_3_ Directing   _4_ Influencing   _1_ Steady   _2_ Cautious

2. Total the numbers in each of the four columns. When all four columns are added together, they will equal 50.

Column 1	Column 2	Column 3	Column 4
4 Directing	3 Influencing	2 Steady	2 Cautious
3 Decisive	4 Optimistic	1 Patient	2 Restrained
1 Daring	2 Enthusiastic	3 Stabilizing	4 Analytical
4 Competitive	2 Talkative	3 Accommo-dating	1 Precise
4 Forceful	2 Charming	3 Easygoing	1 Curious
16 Total	13 Total	12 Total	9 Total

Interpretation

If your highest column total is under Column 1, you are a Director.

If your highest column total is under Column 2, you are a Socializer.

If your highest column total is under Column 3, you are a Relater.

If your highest column total is under Column 4, you are a Thinker.

The Director: Look at My Accomplishments!

Goals and Fears

Directors, driven by an inner need to lead and be in personal control, take charge of people and situations. They want to reach their own goals. Because their key need is to achieve, Directors seek no-nonsense, bottom-line results. Their motto is: "Lead, follow, or get out of the way." They want to win, so they challenge people or rules. Similarly, Directors also accept challenges, take authority, and go headfirst into solving problems.

Closely related to Directors' goals are their fears: falling into a routine, being taken advantage of, and looking "soft." Therefore, they may go to extremes to prevent those fears from materializing. Directors may appear impatient, but they make things happen.

Strengths and Weaknesses

Because Directors need to have control, they like to take the lead in both business and social settings. The song "Don't Fence Me In" may have been written for this type; they behave almost as if they were claustrophobic if they believe someone is trying to stymie them. As natural renegades, Directors want to satisfy their need for autonomy. They want things done their way or no way at all.

Directors often show strong directive management and operational tendencies; they work quickly and impressively by themselves. People of this type try to shape their environments to overcome obstacles to their accomplishments. They demand maximum freedom to manage themselves and others, using their leadership skills to become winners. Additionally, Directors often have good administrative and delegation skills: If they could delegate their exercise regimens or visits to the dentist's office, they probably would.

These assertive types tend to appear cool, independent, and competitive. Directors opt for measurable results, including their personal worth, as determined by individual track records. Of all the types, they like and initiate changes the most. The lion symbolizes this personality type—leaders and authorities, with the inner desires to be number one.

Less positive Director components include stubbornness, impatience, and toughness. Because they naturally prefer to take control of others, they may have a low tolerance for the feelings, attitudes, and "inadequacies" of coworkers, subordinates, friends, families, and romantic interests.

Directors process data conceptually by using deductive reasoning—from general to specific information. They are more comfortable using the left brain than the right. Understanding how they process data helps us to better understand the emphasis on bottom-line results.

They may use various "mind control" techniques to help them focus on one task priority at a time. For instance, some Directors are adept at blocking out distractions when they immerse themselves in projects. They do not hear voices, sirens, or doorbells, and channel all their energies into specific jobs.

Under pressure, Directors are likely to rid themselves of anger by ranting, raving, or challenging others. They naturally react to tense situations with a fight response. This tendency reflects the Directors' natural blind spots concerning other people's views and feelings. Although this venting allows the relief of their own inner tensions and hostilities, other personality types may feel intimidated by this stress-reducing practice. But the Directors' barks usually exceed their bites, and they may soon forget what specifically upset them in the first place.

Director musicians and performers typically seek to simultaneously command the stage and awe their audiences. They envision themselves rising above their admirers and peers and moving into the position of number one, the best ever. People in this competitive category welcome all challengers. As Vince Lombardi, the former coach of the Green Bay Packers football team, once said, "Winning isn't everything; it's the only thing."

As an overview, Directors tend to have the following qualities:

- **Take charge.** They naturally seek direct control and want to run things their own way.

- **Control oriented.** They fear losing personal power or status.

- **Competitive.** They want to win.

- **Motivated to be number one.** They seek to be first or "on top" whether other people approve or not.

- **Task focused.** They strive to get the job done, often seeming oblivious to others' feelings.

- **Achievers.** They view life in terms of overcoming obstacles to success.

- **Strong willed.** Once they make up their minds, they prefer to stick to their ideas, even to the point of becoming headstrong, especially under stress.

✠ **Dealing With Directors** ✠

Directors' Characteristics	So You...
Care about being number one	—Show them new opportunities and how to win
Think logically	—Display reasoning
Want facts and highlights	—Provide concise data
Strive for results	—Agree on goals and boundaries, then support or get out of their way
Like personal choices	—Allow them to "do their thing," within limits
Like changes	—Vary routines
Prefer to delegate	—Look for opportunities to modify their work-load focus
Want others to notice accomplishments	—Compliment them on what they have done
Need to be in charge	—Let them take the lead, when appropriate, but give them parameters
Tend toward conflict	—If necessary, argue with conviction on points of disagreement, backed up with facts; don't argue on the basis of "personality"

- **Impatient.** They expect other people to help them get results, now!

- **Busy.** They often involve themselves with many projects simultaneously, sometimes to the point of "workaholism."

The Socializer: Hey, Look at Me!

Goals and Fears

Outgoing, open Socializers like to go where the action is. Typically, they are outwardly energetic or fast-paced, and relationships tend to naturally take priority over tasks. Socializers try to influence others in optimistic, friendly ways focused on positive outcomes, whether in the social or work environment. In other words, Socializers believe that if they show others that they like them, then the others will be more likely to reciprocate by responding favorably. Because recognition and approval motivate them, they often move in and around the limelight and hub of activity.

Socializers want your admiration and thrive on acknowledgment, compliments, and applause. "It's not just whether you win or lose; it's how you look when you play the game." People's admiration and acceptance typically mean more to Socializers than to any other type. If you are not talking about them, Socializers may spend a considerable amount of time talking about themselves to gain the acceptance they want. Their biggest fear is public humiliation—whether appearing uninvolved, unattractive, unsuccessful, or unacceptable to others. These frightening forms of social rejection threaten the Socializers' core needs for approval. Consequently, they may go to extremes to avoid public humiliation, lack of inclusion, or loss of social recognition.

Strengths and Weaknesses

Socializers' primary strengths are their enthusiasm, persuasiveness, and friendliness. They are idea people who can get others caught up in their dreams. With great persuasion, they influence others and shape their environments by building alliances to accomplish results. Then they seek nods and comments of approval and recognition for those results. If compliments do not come, Socializers may invent their own. "Well, Chris, I just feel like patting myself on the back today for a job well done!" They are stimulating, talkative, and communicative. Porpoises would be good symbols for Socializers—playful, sociable, and talkative.

Natural weaknesses of Socializers include too much involvement, impatience, fear of being alone, and short attention spans. These weaknesses cause them to become easily bored. With even a little data in, Socializers tend to make generalizations. They may not check everything out, assuming someone else will do it; other times they procrastinate because redoing something just is not exciting enough. When Socializers feel that they do not have enough stimulation and involvement, they get bored and look for something new again...and again...and again. Taken to extremes, their behaviors can appear superficial, haphazard, erratic, and too emotional.

If they pursue the entertainment field for careers, Socializers typically allow their natural, animated emotions to show and to flow. They become stimulated by the movement and reactions of the audience, trying to get the audience to figuratively fall in love with them by acting charming and friendly. They want viewers to feel, "He (or she) is fabulous!"

As an overview, Socializers tend to have the following qualities:

- **Optimistic.** They prefer to view the positives in life and often block out negative situations, facts, and concerns.

- **Fast paced.** They talk, move, and do most activities quickly.

- **Emotional.** They readily show their own feelings and respond to others' feelings.

- **Approval seeking.** They look to others for acceptance and reenergizing; they want people to approve of and like one another.

- **Fun loving.** They seek an upbeat, positive, casual atmosphere and love a good party, especially with friends.

- **Excitable.** They show emotions and become enthusiastic (at best) or rattled (at worst).

- **Spontaneous.** They behave impulsively and dislike planning or having to deal with follow-through details.

- **Expressive.** At times, they may forget and divulge confidential information or say too much to the wrong people.

⊕ **Dealing With Socializers** ⊕

Socializers' Characteristics	So You...
Care about approval and appearances	—Show them that you admire and like them
Seek enthusiastic people and situations	—Behave optimistically and provide upbeat setting
Think emotionally	—Support their feelings when possible
Want to know the general expectations	—Avoid involved details, focus on the "big picture"
Need involvement and people contact	—Interact and participate with them
Like changes and innovations	—Vary the routine; avoid requiring long-term repetition from them
Want others to notice them	—Compliment them personally and often
Need help often to get organized	—Do it together
Dislike conflict	—Act nonaggressively and avoid arguing directly on personal basis
Look for action and stimulation	—Keep up a fast, lively, pace
Surround themselves with optimism	—Support their ideas and do not shatter their dreams; show them your positive side
Want feedback that they "look good"	—Mention their accomplishments, progress, and your genuine appreciation

The Relater: Notice How Well-Liked I Am

Goals and Fears

People of this type want respect, proven by your sincere personal attention and acceptance of them. Steadiness and follow-through actions characterize these people. They prefer a slower and easier pace: "It's not whether you win or lose...it's the teamwork and friendship that counts." They focus on building trust and getting acquainted because they aim for longstanding personal relationships. Pushy, aggressive behavior irritates them.

Relaters strive for security. Their goal is to maintain the stability they prefer in a relatively constant environment. To Relaters, although the unknown may be an intriguing concept, they prefer to stick with what they already know and have experienced. "Risk" is an ugly word to Relaters. They favor more measured actions, like keeping things as they have been and are, even if the present situation happens to be unpleasant. Related to their goal of keeping things very similar is their accompanying fear of change and disorganization. Consequently, any disruption in their routine patterns can cause distress in Relaters. Fearing sudden changes, they are naturally concerned with what may happen. A general worry is that the unknown may be even more unpleasant than the present. Relaters need to think about and plan for changes. Finding sameness within change minimizes their stress by identifying the specific assurances required to cope with such demands.

Strengths and Weaknesses

Relaters naturally "wear well" and are an easy type to get along with. They prefer stable relationships that do not jeopardize anyone, especially themselves. Koalas are appropriate symbols for Relaters; they share a slow, steady pace; relaxed disposition; and the appearance of approachability and warmth.

Relaters tend to plan and follow through. This helps them to routinely plug along. However, they have their own unique difficulties with speaking up; they tend to go along with others or conditions, despite inwardly disagreeing. More assertive types might take advantage of Relaters' tendencies to give in and to avoid confrontation. Additionally, Relaters' reluctance to express themselves can result in hurt feelings. Lack of assertiveness can take its toll on Relaters' health and well-being.

Relaters yearn for more tranquility and security in their lives than the other types. They often act pleasant and cooperative, but seldom incorporate emotional extremes such as rage and euphoria in their behavioral repertoire. Unlike Socializers, Relaters usually experience less dramatic or frequently-occurring peaks and valleys to their more moderate emotional state. This reflects their natural need for composure, stability, and balance.

Relater celebrities tend to give predictable deliveries. Both the audience and performer may seem to merge because Relaters feel so in tempo with their viewers. Typical audience responses may include: "He's truly one of us!" Or, "It's like being with a member of the family or my closest friend!" Relaters welcome group participation, and their performances reflect their natural give-and-take.

⊕ **Dealing With Relaters** ⊕

Relaters' Characteristics	So You...
Care about stability	—Show how your idea minimizes risk
Think logically	—Show reasoning
Want documentation and facts	—Provide data and proof
Like personal involvement	—Demonstrate your interest in them as people
Need to know step-by-step sequences	—Provide outline and/or detailed instructions as you personally "walk them through"
Want others to notice their patient perseverance	—Compliment for their steady follow-through
Avoid risks/changes	—Give them personal assurances
Dislike conflict	—Act nonaggressively, focusing on common interests or the support that is needed
Accommodate others	—Allow them to provide service or support for others
Look for calmness and peace	—Provide a relaxing, friendly atmosphere
Enjoy teamwork	—Provide them with a cooperative group
Want sincere feedback that they are appreciated	—Acknowledge their easygoing manner and helpful efforts, when appropriate

As an overview, Relaters tend to have the following qualities:

- **Easygoing.** They show calm, measured, low-key behaviors and outlooks.

- **Slower paced.** They wait until they know the steps or guidelines before acting, then they move forward in a methodical manner.

- **Diplomatic.** They define themselves by their desire for stable relationships with others and often view problems or concerns as workable.

- **Predictable.** They favor routine and stable conditions and practices.

- **Persevering.** They are likely to stick to a project for long periods of time or at least until the concrete results have been produced.

- **Modest.** They are not likely to "blow their own horns," but appreciate it when others sincerely acknowledge their contributions.

- **Accommodating.** They like to get along with others through predictable role relationships.

- **Neighborly.** They prefer friendly, pleasant, helpful working relationships.

The Thinker: Have You Noticed My Efficiency?

Goals and Fears

Thinkers concern themselves more with content than with congratulations. They prefer involvement with

products and services under specific, preferably controlled, conditions so the process and the results can be
correct. Because their primary concern is accuracy, human emotions may take a back seat with people of this
type. After all, emotions are subjective and tend to distort
objectivity. Thinkers' biggest fears—uncontrolled emotions and irrational acts—relate to their goals. More precisely, Thinkers fear that these illogical acts may prevent
goal achievement. Similarly, they fear emotionality and
irrationality in others. This type strives to avoid embarrassment, so they attempt to control both themselves and
their emotions.

Strengths and Weaknesses

Thinkers' strengths include accuracy, dependability, in-
dependence, clarification and testing skills, follow-
through, and organization. They often focus on
expectations (such as policies, practices, and procedures)
and outcomes. They want to know how things work so
they can evaluate how correctly they function. Foxes are
appropriate symbols for Thinkers—cagey, resourceful,
and careful. Because they need to be right, they prefer
checking processes themselves. This tendency toward
perfectionism, taken to an extreme, can result in "paraly-
sis by overanalysis." These overly cautious traits may
result in worry that the process is not progressing properly; this further promotes their tendency to behave in
more critical, detached ways.

Thinkers prefer clearly defined priorities and a
known pace that is agreeable to them (especially when
task time lines and deadlines are involved); they prioritize
tasks over people. Other types typically live life through

a single predominant time orientation—past, present, or future. But Thinkers are apt to be concerned about all three as one aspect of their complex mental makeup. They tend to see the serious sides of situations as well as the lighter sides; this accounts for their natural mental wit.

Thinkers concentrate on making decisions in both logical and cautious ways to ensure that they take the best available action. "It's not whether you win or lose...it's how you play the game"—the more technically perfect, the better.

Because they comply with personal standards, Thinkers demand a lot from themselves and others and may succumb to overly critical tendencies. But Thinkers often keep their criticisms to themselves, hesitating to tell people what they think is deficient. They typically share information, both positive and negative, only on a "need-to-know" basis when they are assured that there will be no negative consequences for themselves.

When Thinkers quietly hold their ground, they do so because of their proven knowledge of facts and details or their evaluation that others will react less assertively. They can be assertive when they perceive they are in control of a relationship or their environment. Having figured out the specific risks, margins of error, and other variables that significantly influence the desired results, they will take action.

Thinker entertainers want to move beyond the audience, because they want to deliver a one-of-a-kind, captivating, near-perfect performance. They want spectators to think, "What a unique performance!" or "Nothing else is quite like it!" When they take their varied stages, Thinker entertainers have meticulously prepared themselves to provide a memorable experience with each intense performance; for this reason, Thinkers seem more emotionally drained from their efforts than other types of entertainers.

As an overview, Thinkers tend to have the following qualities:

- **Careful.** They are methodical, cautious, and do not jump into things quickly.

- **Precise.** They need to be accurate, so they check and recheck, trying to find the right or best available answer

- **Proper.** They are more formal, discreet, and inclined to allow others to be in their own space, expecting the same for themselves.

- **Private.** They keep their thoughts to themselves and do not willingly disclose their own or others' thoughts and feelings.

- **Reserved.** They appear somewhat formal and cool; it takes time to get to know them, and they have fewer close relationships than other types.

- **Logical.** They are inclined to be process-oriented seekers of reason.

- **Inventive.** They like to see things in new ways and often have a unique perspective that includes or addresses both themselves and others.

- **Contemplative.** They are introverted and reflective, pondering both the "why" and "how" elements in situations.

⊕ **Dealing With Thinkers** ⊕

Thinkers' Characteristics	So You...
Dislike aggressive approaches	—Approach them in an indirect, nonthreatening way
Think logically	—Show your reasoning
Seek data	—Give it to them in writing
Need to know the process	—Provide explanations and rationale
Utilize caution	—Allow them to think, inquire, and check before they make decisions
Prefer to do things themselves	—Let them check on others' progress and performance when they delegate
Want others to notice their accuracy	—Compliment them on their thoroughness and correctness when appropriate
Gravitate toward quality control	—Let them assess and be involved in the process when possible
Avoid conflict	—Ask tactfully for the clarification and assistance you may need
Need to be right	—Allow them time to find the best or "correct" answer, within available limits
Like to contemplate	—Tell them "why" and "how"

Four Types, Just Acting Themselves

With the natural differences among the four behavioral types in mind, pretend that you want to give four people fifteen to twenty minutes to make three simple decisions:

- Where the next meeting will take place

- When it will happen

- The theme of the meeting

Quite by accident, your group consists of one Relater, one Thinker, one Director, and one Socializer who all believe in practicing the Golden Rule. Do you think they will get the job done? Perhaps, or perhaps not, depending on how each responds in handling the simple task.

Let's see why this may not work out. As they walk into the room, the Director typically speaks first. "Here's my plan...." The Socializer says, "Hey! Who died and left you boss?" The Thinker says, "You know there is more to this than we thought. We might want to consider other relevant issues and break into subcommittees to explore them." The Relater smiles and says, "We may not get this done if we don't work as a team like we have before."

On the other hand, consider putting all four of one behavioral type into a room to make those decisions. They would get the job done, would they not? Not if they follow the Golden Rule verbatim!

What do you call it when you send four Directors into the same room? War!

Or four Thinkers? A laundry list full of questions!

And four Relaters? Nothing! They sit around smiling at each other: "You go first." "No, why don't you go first? By the way, how's the family?"

When four Socializers walk out, try asking them if they have gotten the job done. "Get what done?" They have had a party and instead come out with ten new jokes and stories.

We may be exaggerating to make a point, but in some cases not by much. Directors tend to have the assertiveness and leadership initiative to get tasks started. They may then delegate to others for follow-through, enabling the Directors to start still other new projects that interest them more.

Planning and organizational tendencies motivate Thinkers. If you want a task done precisely, find a Thinker. Of the four types, they are the most motivated to be correct—the quality-control experts.

Relaters have persistence, patience, follow-through, people-to-people strengths, and responsiveness. People with problems may choose to go to a sympathetic appearing Relater because he or she listens, empathizes, and reacts to their feelings.

Socializers are natural entertainers who thrive on involvement with people. They also love to start things, but often do not finish them. In fact, they may pick up three balls, throw them in the air, and yell "Catch!" Emotional, enthusiastic, optimistic, and friendly, Socializers usually pep up an otherwise dull environment.

⊕ **The Four Types** ⊕

Task-Oriented Types

Thinkers

Directors

People-Oriented Types

Relaters

Socializers

Faster-Paced Types

Directors

Socializers

Slower-Paced Types

Relaters

Thinkers

What They Seek

Directors......................................Power and Control

Socializers...................................Popularity and Prestige

Relaters..Sincerity and Appreciation

Thinkers.......................................Accuracy and Precision

How They Make Decisions

Director..Decisive

Socializer.....................................Spontaneous

Relater...Conferring

Thinker ....Deliberate

Pick a Type...Any Type

After this general introduction to the four core behavioral types, you probably already know which one is most like you. When you are yourself, your core behavioral type shows.

Each of us has his or her own natural behavioral style, whether it be Director, Socializer, Relater, or Thinker. Behavioral style is most evident in those recurring verbal, vocal, and visual habits that we use to deal with people and to work at tasks. It is our most comfortable way of behaving most of the time. This pattern is most often observed outside of the workplace, when we have no other expectations on ourselves. One interesting way to determine your natural behavior pattern would be to describe your ideal vacation experience.

Did you also recognize other people you know? Beyond deciding which type is most like you, you may have thought of people who sounded quite similar to one or more of the personality types in this chapter—those you harmonize with and those who tend to "rub you the wrong way." Now that you know which type you are, you can better determine other people's types. Integrating what you know about yourself with what you can observe and learn about others reveals valuable information to help you relate more effectively with them.

However, we all have *acquired* behavioral styles as well. Only 15 percent of the entire population can be understood clearly through just these four styles. Most of us have a secondary style that we have acquired in response to our life experiences. These acquired styles are often used by people in their work lives in response to the types of expectations required for satisfactory job performance. This second tendency often helps people to function more effectively in roles that have a greater variety of expectations. It is important to remember that at any one point in time—especially when under stress—one style will predominate.

Acquired style then can be thought of as one's "second nature," which includes those additional tendencies that most people have added to their core styles. These mixed-style combinations of sixteen patterns are shown on the Master Chart of Mixed Styles. The primary drive, which describes a person's desired end result, is listed in the first column. Each row describes four varieties of a certain style; for example, a Director can be a pure Director, a Socializing Director (Adventurer), a Relating Director (Producer), or a Thinking Director (Pioneer).

For further information about these patterns and how to assess them with input from yourself and others, we recommend that you refer to the *Behavioral Profiles* instruments, available from Pfeiffer & Company.[1]

The next chapter explains how to figure out others' personality types by focusing on specific verbal, vocal, and visual signals they provide.

---

[1] Pfeiffer & Company, 8517 Production Avenue, San Diego, California 92121 (800-274-4434).

⊕ **Master Chart of Mixed Styles** ⊕

Primary Drive (Desired End Result)	Secondary Approach (Personal Style/Processes)			
	Directing	*Socializing*	*Relating*	*Thinking*
Director: Power & Control	Director	Adventurer	Producer	Pioneer
Socializer: Popularity & Prestige	Enthusiast	Socializer	Helper	Impresser
Relater: Stability & Appreciation	Go-getter	Harmonizer	Relater	Specialist
Thinker: Privacy & Precision	Mastermind	Assessor	Perfecter	Thinker

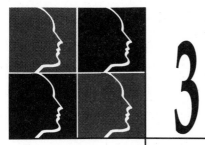

3

Recognizing Verbal, Vocal, and Visual Clues

Others' Behavioral Types

Now that you are familiar with your core behavioral type, how can you recognize other types when you meet them? Because relationships depend on appropriate interactions with each behavioral type, the immediate question is, "How can I identify someone's behavioral type, and how can I do it quickly?"

The chart entitled "Dimensions of Openness and Directness" illustrates two important dimensions for recognizing another person's behavioral type: Direct/Indirect and Open/Self-Contained. We all exhibit a range of these characteristics in our expressed, observable behaviors. But we need to focus on how people act in order to determine their core type. It will not do to ask, "Excuse me, but would you mind giving me some information about how Indirect or Direct you are? How Open or Self-Contained are you? I would like to figure out your behavioral type." Neither will it do to guess, but that approach is seldom necessary because people give others many clues. However, you need to know how to recognize these clues. To identify someone's type, observe what he or she does by tuning in to verbal, vocal, and visual behaviors.

Verbal, Vocal, and Visual Clues

The verbal channel of communication includes the words people use to express themselves—the content. Vocal and visual channels, the other two areas, convey the intent of

Dimensions of Openness and Directness

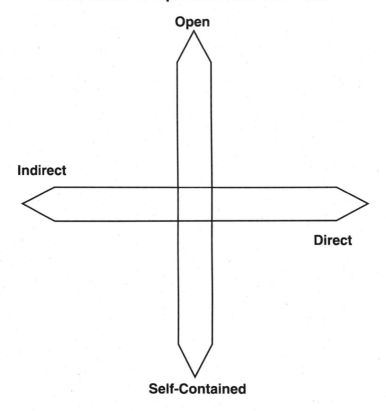

Open

Indirect

Direct

Self-Contained

the message—how people want to say it. The vocal channel includes all the subtle aspects of voice intonation—
volume, speed, resonance, pitch, inflection, and rhythm.
The visual channel includes all the aspects of body language—the range of movements and positions—from the
subtle raising of an eyebrow to the precise movements of
the trained actor.

The following sections outline a range of verbal,
vocal, and visual characteristics that are observable behaviors for each type. But beware! These descriptions
refer to actions you can see, not value judgments you may

be tempted to make about them. If you see someone jumping up and down, that person may be throwing a temper tantrum, may have stepped on a nail, or may feel very excited. All you can say for certain is that the person is jumping up and down. Finding out why requires more observable verbal, vocal, and visual clues.

Is the Person Direct or Indirect?

Directness, the first of two dimensions of expressed behavior, is the amount of involvement a person uses to influence people and situations. Directness means the tendency to move forward or act outwardly by expressing thoughts, feelings, or expectations.

Direct People

Direct people take the social initiative and create a powerful first impression. They tend to be assertive, fast-paced people who make swift decisions and take risks. They can easily become impatient with others who cannot keep up with their pace. As active people who talk a lot, they appear confident and sometimes dominant. Direct people tend to express opinions readily and make emphatic statements. Such individuals try to shape their environments and relationships—"Tell Chris that we have to talk ASAP!"

Direct people move faster, assert themselves more, and act more competitively than indirect people. At worst, these tendencies can transform into hastiness, combativeness, or a lesser awareness of others' needs. People of this type are outspoken, talkative, and dominant extroverts who focus on interests in their environment. In other words—they want action! They tend to work and play faster than indirect people. At social gatherings, they are the ones who introduce themselves to others as a natural way of seeking to influence their surroundings.

They prefer to make rapid decisions and become impatient when things do not move fast enough or do not go their way. Checking for errors is too time-consuming and self-involving for Direct people; they would rather leave that task to others. Instead of checking their facts, they busily rush into the new areas. In fact, they rush into so many new areas that their time seems to evaporate into thin air. This is one reason that they have difficulty consistently being prompt—something always seems to happen. Meanwhile, their more punctual Indirect friends learn to busy themselves with projects or magazines while they wait for their more easily sidetracked companions.

Direct people may enjoy risks and want results now—or yesterday. Risks are a way of life with them. Not only are they less worried than others about rocking the boat, they will often tip it over and splash around in the water. They crave excitement, so they do as much as possible to get it.

Direct people believe most times that quantity beats quality (within limits known only to them). They are likely to tolerate a higher error rate than their Indirect counterparts. Direct people make efforts more often, even if their success ratio is lower. They generally decide that the number of successes is more important than the percentage of successes.

Anyone involved in telemarketing or outside sales realizes that setbacks litter the road to success. Direct people excel in these arenas because they can take "no" for an answer; their answer is simply to go out and find more prospects. Aware that the "yes" answers are out there somewhere, they are determined to unearth them.

Direct people point, finger jab, or otherwise more observably express themselves in methods ranging from open arms to forearms—literally, a hug or a shove. They are verbally intense and emphasize their points of view with confident-sounding vocal intonations and assertive body language.

Direct people speak with conviction. Fast-talking, they like to tell, not ask, about situations. If you want to know the answer, just ask them. They can even become brutally blunt— "That's supposed to be a custom suit? It looks more like a horse blanket."

Impatient and quick-paced, Direct people jump into things; therefore, they get themselves in more tenuous situations than their Indirect counterparts. Just as the songs of the sirens lured sailors to their doom, the windows of opportunity beckon to Direct people. Entering sometimes nets them huge results and sometimes slaps them with dramatic disasters. Wherever their inclinations take them, their natural tendency is to do their own thing.

When the windows of opportunity crack open, the Direct types cannot wait to tell somebody. They seek willing listeners—usually of the Indirect variety—and they say, "I've found a gray area."

But what sort of feedback do you suppose the Indirect types probably provide? "It sounds interesting, but it also raises many questions. Have you asked anyone else for an opinion? Your boss, for instance?" To which the Direct person might respond, "Ask my boss? Forget it!

What if the answer is no? Then what would I do? My hands would be tied."

This more Direct person's motto in these cases is, "It's easier to beg forgiveness than seek permission. When in doubt, do it anyway. You can always apologize later."

Indirect People

On the opposite side of the spectrum, Indirect people are more quiet and reserved. They seem more easygoing. Indirect people ask questions and listen more than they talk. They typically reserve their opinions. When asked to take a stand, they may make tentative statements. They often appear more objective, quiet, and indecisive. When taken to an extreme, these positive traits can appear as negative ones—wishy-washy, tight-lipped, nonassertive behaviors. Indirect people are also less confronting, less demanding, less assertive, and less socially competitive than their Direct counterparts. People of this type tend to be team players who allow others to take the social initiative. For instance, if they want to go somewhere, they might wait for someone to invite them instead of suggesting the idea to others.

Indirect people tend to be more security-conscious; they move slowly, meditate on their decisions, and avoid big risks. As a result, they often refrain from taking bold chances or spontaneous actions. After all, what better way to keep from failing? If you do nothing until you are satisfied that the action will be an improvement, you do only sure things. Those sure things result in a higher success ratio, so they are more natural for Indirect people. The number of successes divided by number of tries equals success. In a given month, Indirect people may try ten things. Nine may be successful, and one not success-ful—for a success ratio of 90 percent.

Indirect people tend to take "no" answers as personal rejections, responding by examining other alternatives that will not force them to go out again. "Maybe if I send out a direct mail letter first, then follow up by phone, I'll increase my chances of getting a 'yes.'"

When Indirect people fail, they tend to take the set-back personally. They are likely to internalize or privately think about it, often wondering if there is something wrong with them. Just give them a hint that something is going wrong, and reserved folks may engage in negative self-talk for days.

Indirect people tend to move at a slower or more measured pace. For them, eventually is good enough. They speak and respond more slowly because they are more cautious or stability focused when considering change. If the behavior becomes too measured, detractors (usually Direct people) can view this as stalling or even lacking interest.

Predictability is important to Indirect people, so they tend to consider the pros and cons, attend to details, and find out the facts. When caught in a gray area with no clear-cut guidelines, they usually ask for clarification or permission before they take action. Indirect people seek to meet their needs by accommodating the requirements of their environment. Generally they operate according to established formats and rules; when you make an ap-pointment with an Indirect person, you can expect that person to show up on time, or possibly be waiting for you!

Indirect people tend to communicate by asking in-stead of stating. Their questions clarify, support, or seek more information—"By that, do you mean...?" They prefer qualified statements—"According to my sources, the candidate received an advanced degree from a nonaccredited university." They speak more tentatively and take a roundabout or step-by-step approach—"It seems to me that this is so." If they do not like something, they respond subtly—"Well, I think your other suit looks better." They reserve the right to express their opinions or keep them to themselves. But, they can also act like impregnable rocks when they do not want to crack.

Think of someone you know who irritates you. Now that you know about Direct and Indirect characteristics, can you decide which trait best describes him or her? One important consideration is to determine the person's preferred pace. Pace refers to natural rate of speed—whether the person does things quickly or slowly. Bearing in mind pace and other trait descriptors for Direct and Indirect people, decide whether that person is more Direct or Indirect. It is important to realize that people vary as to where they fall on the Direct/Indirect scale.

You may be wondering which are better—Direct traits or Indirect ones. We can answer with an unqualified answer: "It depends." Sometimes it is better to act more Direct and sometimes it is better to act more Indirect. Comparing the two is like evaluating San Diego and New York City. Each is very different, yet we could build a strong argument in either one's favor.

Appropriateness depends on the requirements of a situation. The real question is not which approach is better but how to best use the positive aspects of each trait while recognizing the less-developed attributes that accompany it. Because each of our lives involves a variety of situations

Summary of Direct and Indirect Behaviors

Directness is how a person deals with information and situations.

Indirect Behaviors

Approaching risk, decisions, or change slowly and cautiously
Contributing infrequently to group conversations
Using gestures and vocal intonation infrequently
Making qualified statements often (e.g., "I think so")
Emphasizing points with explanations of content
Asking questions for clarification, support, or information
Reserving expression of opinions
Being patient, cooperative, and diplomatic
Waiting for others to introduce themselves
Shaking hands gently
Making intermittent eye contact
Following established rules and policies

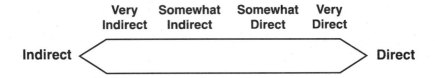

	Very Indirect	Somewhat Indirect	Somewhat Direct	Very Direct	
Indirect					**Direct**

Direct Behaviors

Approaching risk, decisions, or change quickly or spontaneously
Contributing frequently to group conversations
Using gestures and vocal intonation frequently
Making emphatic statements often (e.g., "I'm certain")
Emphasizing points with voice and body language
Asking questions rhetorically
Offering opinions readily
Being less patient, more competitive, and confronting
Introducing oneself
Shaking hands firmly
Making sustained eye contact
Bending established rules and policies

requiring differing responses, there is no one best personality type. The idea is to maximize people's natural traits while understanding and trying to minimize their accompanying drawbacks.

Is the Person Open or Self-Contained?

In addition to either Direct or Indirect behaviors, people also tend to be either Open or Self-Contained—the other major dimension that describes people's daily actions. Directness and Indirectness describe people's observable behaviors—how others see and hear them behaving. The second behavioral scale explains the motivating goal behind these daily actions—why people do the things they do in the ways they do them. When combined, these scales indicate two aspects: (1) how much a person reveals his or her own thoughts and feelings, and (2) how much he or she supports other people's expressions of their thoughts and feelings.

Open People (Supporting)

People who talk with their bodies, use more vocal inflection, make continual eye contact, and speak in terms of feelings project more Open than Self-Contained behaviors. Other Open cues that show greater responsiveness include animated facial expressions, much hand and body movement, a flexible time perspective, and immediate nonverbal feedback. Open people also like to tell stories and anecdotes and make personal contact.

Open people are more likely to respond to digressions than are people with Self-Contained personalities. They need to make conversation more enjoyable, so they look favorably on straying from the subject to discuss personal experiences. As long as something is somewhat related, it probably is relevant—and exaggeration of details just adds interest by fully depicting their experiences.

Open types are also more negotiable about time than Self-Contained types. Their time perspective is organized around the needs of people first and tasks second, so they are more flexible about how others use their time than are Self-Contained types.

Of course, like any behavior that gets overused, these same Open characteristics can also annoy people if they get out of hand. For example, self-disclosure can turn into neediness, digression to inattention, animation to melodrama, acquiescence to weakness, and friendliness to patronizing behavior. As with any tendency, too much of anything can become a liability.

Self-Contained People (Controlling)

If Open types can be described as open books, then Self-Contained ones can be described as more poker faced. Self-Contained individuals prefer to be more guarded and reserved—increasing the probability of gaining an advantage and decreasing the probability of appearing foolish. They usually like to keep their distance, both physically and mentally. Self-Contained people do not touch you and do not like to be touched. You must become acquainted with them by breaking through their exterior shells. Consequently, Self-Contained people tend to stand far away from you, even when shaking hands. They also have a strong sense of personal space and territory.

Self-Contained people show little facial expression, use controlled hand and body movements, and follow a more time-disciplined agenda. People of this type push for facts and details, focus on the issues and tasks at hand, and keep their personal feelings private. Unlike their Open counterparts, they give little nonverbal feedback.

Self-Contained types place high priority on getting things done. They prefer working with things or through people—rather than with or for people. Two characteristic comments in this pattern would be "I can't talk now, Robin. I have a two o'clock deadline to meet" or "I'll let you know when I have time to do that."

Self-Contained people like structure because they expect results within that structured environment. When negatively motivated, these types of individuals can be viewed as coercive, restrictive, or overbearing. They prefer to stick with an agenda, preferably their own agenda. As more naturally independent workers, they need to control the conditions around their tasks—either in terms of input and output (Directness) or the process itself (Indirectness). These Self-Contained people make use of either key talent or key procedures to meet their goals. Thus, they view the planning and supervision processes as ways to reach goals. Direct, Self-Contained individuals need to control people; and Indirect, Self-Contained people need to control their environment.

Because time equals money to Self-Contained people, they are disciplined about how other people use their time. In part, this explains their tendency not to show, discuss, or willingly listen to thoughts and feelings in the ways that Open individuals do. Self-Contained individuals are more matter-of-fact and have more fixed expectations of people and situations. Just as facts place second for Open people, feelings are secondary to those who are more Self-Contained. You might say that Open people experience life by tuning in to the concerns or feeling states (of themselves and others) and then reacting to them. Self-Contained people focus on the points or ideas in question.

Self-Contained people like to know where a conversation is going; idle, nondirected chatter is not for them. If Open types stray from the subject at hand, Self-Contained people find a way to bring them back on track. They usually need clarity before they move on to the next topic. If you get off the subject, they are likely to ask, "Can you sum that up for me?" or, "What is the key point you're trying to make?"

Because of their different priorities, Self-Contained types can perceive more Open ones as time-wasting or wishy-washy people. Open people then may view the Self-Contained as cold, unsympathetic, or self-involved. As a result, misunderstandings can quickly grow out of proportion when people do not discern and respond to these types of differences. You may wonder which is better—Open or Self-Contained behavior? Again, the answer is, "It depends." As with Directness and Indirectness, the circumstances at hand determine the appropriateness of any type of behavior. Awareness of potential pitfalls for each personality pattern can save scores of problems for ourselves and others as well as for our coworkers, social groups, and organizations.

Whereas Open people may feel any attention is better than no attention at all, Self-Contained people tend to be more selective about the people with whom they associate. They feel more comfortable retaining firm control over their emotions.

Summary of Open and Self-Contained Behaviors

Open

**Very
Open**

**Somewhat
Open**

**Somewhat
Self-Contained**

**Very
Self-Contained**

Self-Contained

Open Behaviors (Supporting)

Showing and sharing feelings freely
Making decisions based on feelings
Digressing in conversations
Preferring to work with others
Initiating and accepting physical contact
Being easy to get to know
Appearing relaxed and warm
Shaking hands in a friendly manner
Giving a great deal of nonverbal feedback
Responding to dreams, visions, and
    concepts
Showing a great deal of enthusiasm
Being flexible about how time is used by
    others

Self-Contained Behaviors (Controlling)

Showing and sharing feelings in a guarded
    fashion
Making decisions based on evidence
Focusing on issues and tasks in
    conversations
Preferring to work independently
Avoiding or minimizing physical contact
Being harder to get to know
Appearing reserved and proper
Shaking hands in a formal manner
Giving very little nonverbal feedback
Responding to realities, experiences, and
    facts
Showing not much enthusiasm
Being disciplined about how time is used
    by others

When the chips are down, Open people tend to spare others' feelings at the expense of completing tasks. Self-Contained types want to get things done, even though feelings may get hurt as part of the emotional cost of accomplishment. This does not necessarily mean that Open types do not believe in responsibly doing their work; it just means that people are of higher concern. Similarly, it does not mean that Self-Contained people do not value other people; they simply think the best way to deal with people is by a more controlled style of behavior.

Identifying Styles

The four behavioral styles—Director, Socializer, Relater, and Thinker—can be charted according to the dimensions of Direct/Indirect and Open/Self-Contained. Directors fall in the quadrant that represents both Direct and Self-Contained (Controlling); Socializers can be categorized as both Direct and Open (Supporting); Relaters tend to be Indirect and Open (Supporting); and Thinkers would be represented as Indirect and Self-Contained (Controlling).

To identify a person's behavioral style, simply use the process of elimination. If the person is more Direct than Indirect, then you can eliminate the Relater and Thinker types (the two Indirect styles). If the person is more Open than Self-Contained, then eliminate the Director (the more Self-Contained type). Now you arrive at the remaining style, in this case, a Socializer.

Which Type Is This?

You have an appointment with a client whose secretary sets the time for exactly 10:10 A.M. After your client ac-

The Four Behavioral Styles

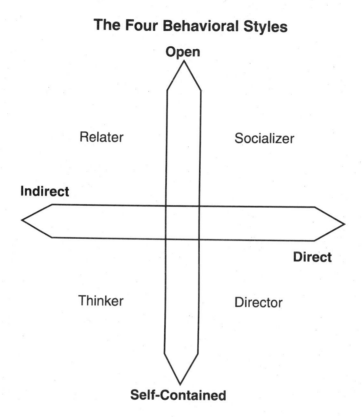

knowledges you in the reception area with a fixed, polite smile, she gives several detailed instructions to her secretary. Gathering behavioral clues, you notice that she dresses impeccably. She again smiles politely at you and asks you to follow her into the office. She tells you where to sit, checks her watch, and says, "You have exactly 15 minutes. Go."

During your presentation, the client remains as expressionless as a statue in a museum. No emotion shows. She asks for highly specific facts, assesses your responses, and then extends the discussion in areas of interest to her. After inviting you to stay longer, she literally closes the sale herself when you give her specific answers to her time, schedule, and cost questions.

There are many clues to help you determine the behavioral style of this client. First, look at her Direct versus Indirect behaviors. You can be fairly sure of placing her

Identifying a Person's Behavioral Style

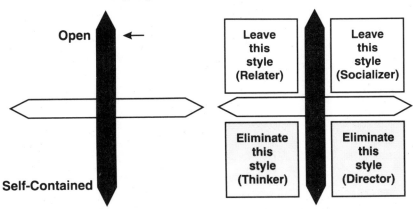

If: The person being observed → **Then:** Eliminate the Thinker and the Director
appears very Open. . . styles (the two Self-Contained styles).

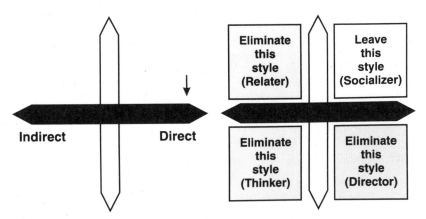

Then If: The person being observed → **Then:** Eliminate the Relater style
appears very Direct, rather (the more indirect of the two
than Indirect. . . remaining styles). The person
is probably a Socializer.

as Direct: She directs the conversation, confronts the issues head-on, controls both you and the situation (when to begin, where to sit, what to discuss), and closes the sale herself. That's Directness! Next, look at her Open or Self-Contained tendencies. By nature of her time discipline, fact and task orientation, formality, and expressionless face, she is fairly easily to classify as Self-Contained.

When you put together the two aspects that determine behavioral style, you have a combined rating of Direct and Self-Contained. These two classifications tell you that the client is a Director.

One More Time

You are conducting a seminar that begins at 8:30 A.M., following an 8:00 A.M. coffee-and-doughnut session. When you arrive at 7:45 A.M., the first participant is already seated in the room, with notepad and pencils lying in front of her. She says nothing until you approach, and then she politely shakes hands. She is totally noncommittal. You ask a few questions and receive polite, short answers.

About 8:15 A.M., with several other people in the room, a person stops hesitantly at the door and softly asks, "Excuse me. Is this the training seminar for salespeople?" When he hears, "Yes," he breathes a sigh, walks in, takes a cup of coffee, and mentions how interesting and helpful he hopes the seminar will be. He asks a few questions and listens intently to others' remarks. He expresses some concern about role playing in front of a group.

At this moment, another participant strides in and asks, "Hey, is this the sales seminar?" When told "Yes," this person dramatizes relief, asks about coffee, and explains that he can't function without that "black poison." He has overheard the comments about role playing and leaps in on the conversation to say how much he likes doing those things. After this remark, he goes on with a tale of how he embarrassed himself in the last role-play session he attended.

Which style is the first person? The second? The last?

The first person's apparent disinterest in conversation and restrained gestures identify her as Indirect. This narrows the possible choices to either Relater or Thinker. She is also clearly in control of her emotions and the setting, making her Self-Contained as opposed to Open. An Indirect/Self-Contained person is a Thinker.

The second participant speaks with a soft voice, requests clarification, and hesitates before starting the seminar. All these clues add up to an Indirect behavior pattern (Thinker or Relater). He volunteers information about personal feelings and gives rapid feedback with his sighs and comments. These are Open characteristics. This person shows a Relater style.

Participant number three demonstrates Directness through his speed of response, fast movements, and high quantity of conversation (Director or Socializer). He also shows Open behaviors by telling stories and responding quickly. These are traits of the Socializer.

The next chapter will describe each style in greater detail and will offer suggestions for recognizing each one in office settings by taking note of their observable characteristics.

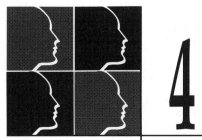

4

How Will You Know One When You Meet One at the Office?

The Director at the Office

When you enter Directors' offices, look around. The general tone suggests authority and control. Projects and papers cover their desks, but they are stacked in neat piles. Both their in- and out-baskets typically bulge with work. They tend to surround themselves with trophies, awards, and other evidence of personal achievement. Virtually everything about the place suggests hustle, bustle, formality, and power. This type is the one that often favors large chairs behind massive authority structures known as power desks. Besides nonverbally announcing, "I'm important," such a desk separates them from visitors, literally keeping them at a distance.

Notice the Walls

In Directors' offices, the walls may include diplomas, commendations, and other evidence of success. One wall may have a large planning sheet or calendar on it to keep track of the many projects being juggled. If Directors have family photos on the wall, they will be hung somewhere out of direct view. To people of this type, offices are places of business; the fewer distractions they have, the better.

Observable Characteristics

Directors like constant activity, so you will seldom catch them idle. Between existing tasks, they pick up new ones. They perk up when competing and appear to thrive with a pressure-cooker schedule. People of this type often squeeze you in on their calendars; they let you know that their time is limited, often very directly. At other times, they signal how busy they are by shifting their gaze elsewhere or by making and taking phone calls while you sit and wait.

They walk fast in pursuit of a tangible goal; Directors may not even notice the people around them. They often act both brisk and brusque without realizing it. Under stress, their impatience emerges, and they may push others aside to reach their goals—completing a report, getting served first, or running out the door to make an appointment. When pressure intensifies, Directors often rise to the occasion. But when they face time constraints, Directors may give in to impatience and rely on educated guesses or hunches rather than facts.

Directors tend to dress comfortably and typically pay less attention to appearance than the other types. Because they program themselves primarily for results, wardrobe may play a secondary role in many fields of work. Directors may be candidates for a timesaving personal shopper or tailor who can choose or measure outfits for them in the privacy of their own offices. People of this type gravitate toward authority symbols, so they may wear navy blue or gray power suits. Directors may like to let people know they've made it without having to tell anyone about it, so they often prefer possessions that symbolize success and authority messages.

Telephone Clues

When you speak on the phone to Directors, treat them in the same way you would in a person-to-person contact. Think of the ABC's: Keep it **A**bridged, **B**rief, and **C**oncise.

Observable Characteristics of a Director		
Verbal	**Vocal**	**Visual**
States more than asks	Uses a great deal of vocal variety	Shakes hands firmly
Talks more than listens	Speaks in forceful tones	Makes steady eye contact
Relies on verbal, not written, communication	Communicates readily	Gestures to emphasize points
Makes strong statements	Uses high-volume, rapid speech	Displays impatience
Tends to be blunt and to the point	Uses challenging voice intonations	Uses fast-moving body language

Prepare your delivery with the bottom line in mind: "The trend in your industry is toward computer-generated graphics. The research we've conducted with other type-setters in your area suggests increased profits of 20 to 30 percent over two years. I'd like to meet with you for 10 minutes to show you the numbers and see if this concept interests you."

It's not unusual for Directors to call someone and, without saying hello, launch right into the conversation. "You must be kidding; that competitor's shipment will destroy us—by the way, this is Pat." When another person cannot keep up with a Director's speed, that person may be viewed as incompetent.

When you are speaking on the telephone with someone you have not met, decide whether or not the person sends power signals. Directors want to pick the time and place to meet. They often speak in a sort of shorthand—

concisely and pointedly—and sound cool, confident, and demanding. A telephone call from Director Jan sounds like this: "K.C.? Jan. Lee there?" Talking to Directors is like speaking to human telegrams. As commanding speakers who tend not to listen to others, they naturally want to direct the conversation toward their goals. Under stress, they can become defensive and aggressive, attacking others personally to show who is in control. They dislike using emotional terms and prefer sensible thinking terminology. "I think we will implement this plan tomorrow" or "I think this discussion is over."

Clues From Letters

Letters from Directors tend to be brief, forceful, and to the point. They may mention highlights of conversations or materials, but not belabor them. However, Directors may give specific information for you to follow through or raise questions that they want answered now. Even notes and cards take on abbreviated forms and may show little or no indication of feelings. We know more than one Director who signs personal birthday and Christmas cards with no closing, just a name. Relaters and Socializers gravitate more toward closings such as "Warmly," "Fondly," or "Cordially." But Directors, perhaps in trying to get as many things accomplished as possible, tend to opt for brevity.

The Socializer at the Office

When you enter the working areas of Socializers, look around. Even if you have never been to a Socializer's office before, you may recognize it immediately. Remember Oscar Madison? He and other high Socializers may strew paperwork across their desks—or even trail it along the floor. They react to visual stimuli, so they like to have everything where they can see it. Consequently, their desks often look cluttered and disorganized. If anyone asks about how they find anything, they like to say that they're organized in their disorganization.

Notice the Walls

Socializer walls may sport prestigious awards, ranging from liberal arts degrees, motivational or upbeat slogans, generalized personal comments, or stimulating posters. You may see notes posted and taped all over with little apparent forethought. The general decor reflects an open, airy, lively atmosphere, and the furniture arrangement suggests warmth, openness, and contact. Socializers seldom sit behind a desk when they talk. They often opt for comfortable, accessible seating, enabling them to meet the goal of getting to know people better. Socializers prefer to sit next to others at a table or on a sofa so that they can see and hear better and sense the others' responses. They talk a lot and show emotion with both with body language and speech.

Observable Characteristics

Socializers have a natural preference for talking and listening in feeling terms. Unconsciously, they may become uncomfortable when talking to a person who uses thinking words. (The opposite also is true).

They like glitz and pizazz! The way Socializers dress often relates to their need for recognition. Because they like others to notice them, they may dress in the latest style. Socializers like bright colors and unusual clothes that prompt others to compliment them. Many Socializers even prefer negative comments to none at all.

In informal polls taken at our seminars, Socializers rank red as their number one color choice for clothes or sports cars. They like glamour, flash, and excitement, and their purchases often express their preferences.

Observable Characteristics of a Socializer

Verbal	Vocal	Visual
Tells stories and anecdotes	Uses a great deal of inflection	Shakes hands firmly
Shares personal feelings and opinions	Varies the pitch of speech	Uses animated facial expressions
Uses informal speech patterns	Varies vocal quality	Is contact oriented
Has a flexible time perspective	Uses high-volume, rapid speech	Tends to act spontaneously
Digresses during conversations	Has a dramatic quality to speech	Uses many hand and body movements

---

Telephone Clues

"What's up?" or "What's happening?" are usual Socializer opening lines. Socializers are sometimes so animated that their gestures almost transmit over the phone lines. Their varied, emotional vocal inflections/intonations and their colorful choices of words may tend toward exaggeration. The telephone can be a favorite toy that enables them to both prolong conversations and recharge themselves, especially when no one else is physically around. You may also detect background noise when you speak to Socializers of this type. They sometimes turn on the television or radio just for the sound, visual stimulation, and activity.

On the phone, Socializers speak rapidly and emotively. Other styles may more naturally use thinking words, instead. Typically, you will notice a wide range of vocal inflection and intonation and a tendency to want to know your reactions. Socializers liven up conversations with personal anecdotes and may keep you on the phone longer than you had anticipated.

Clues From Letters

Letters, too, can reveal the Socializers behind the correspondence. Often, they overuse exclamation points, underlining, and bold highlighting. You can almost hear them emphasizing those picturesque adjectives and adverbs. Just as Socializers tend to speak in stimulating, energetic ways, so do they write. People of this type may also throw in image-provoking personal anecdotes or references to mutually satisfying experiences. When Socializers finish letters or notes, they may add a postscript (P.S.), a P.P.S., or even a P.P.P.S.

A word of caution: These tendencies may not as readily reveal themselves for Socializers who have learned to tone down their natural flair while conducting business. And it is always possible that they have their secretaries tone down letters before sending them out, especially for Socializers who are more exacting or less animated examples of this behavioral type.

The Relater at the Office

When you enter Relaters' offices, be alert for conservatively framed personal slogans, group photos, serene landscapes and posters, and other personal items. Because Relaters seek close relationships, look around for family pictures and mementos, usually positioned so that they can be seen from the Relater's desk chair. Relaters often favor nostalgic memories of stabilizing experiences and relationships in this increasingly complex world. These remembrances of a pleasant, uncomplicated past allow them to transform their offices into an environment of friendliness and warmth. Relaters prefer to arrange seating in a side-by-side, congenial, cooperative manner. Rather than stay behind their desks, they will typically come out and reach out to their visitors.

Notice the Walls

The educational backgrounds of Relaters often include more specialized areas of attention and interest within their professions. You may also see certificates recognizing volunteer hours spent working with hands-on activities in their communities. Although other behavioral types may contribute in different ways—such as gifts of money—Relaters typically enjoy giving their time for causes about which they feel strongly. Besides the possibilities of meeting potential friends, volunteering also helps to satisfy their need to see for themselves: (1) what really is going on, (2) where they fit into the group effort, and (3) how they can get meaningful, concrete results.

Observable Characteristics

You can recognize Relaters by their natural listening patterns and slower, lower-key delivery. Their questions often focus on concrete topics and experiences. "What did you say the terms for payment were again?" They walk casually, acknowledge others, and sometimes get sidetracked by chance encounters.

Relaters dislike calling attention to themselves, so they tend to wear subdued colors, conservatively cut clothing, and conventional styles. Their cars also reveal these preferences: They often like beige or light blue station wagons or vans, factory-recommended tires, and in the best of all worlds—no horn. To Relaters, using a horn is like yelling.

Observable Characteristics of a Relater		
Verbal	**Vocal**	**Visual**
Asks more than states	Speaks in an even-tempered manner	Shakes hands gently
Listens more than talks	Uses less forceful tones of expression	Uses less animated facial expressions
Reserves opinions	Speaks at a lower, quieter volume	Makes intermittent eye contact
Uses less verbal communication	Uses a slow rate of speech	Exhibits patience
Uses a slow pace	Has a steady quality to speech	Uses slow-moving body language

Telephone Clues

"How are you?" or "I'm glad to hear from you again," are typical Relater greetings. Their warmth can seem to transcend the limitations of the phone lines. Although Relaters prefer more personal interactions with people, they will settle for indirect contact—especially if the person is pleasant and nonthreatening. They project this people orientation through the phone lines and like to build a personal, first-name relationship with callers. Even without knowing you, a Relater may say, "You don't have to be so formal. Just call me Chris." Relaters may project a desire to know you personally or to provide you with good service.

Their steady, even vocal intonations convey friendliness, comfort, and a sense of relaxation. Relaters tend to be naturals at listening to other people's ideas and feelings, whether on the phone or in person. They are interested in the point-by-point description of what you did yesterday or the sequential pattern of how to complete a certain task. You probably are talking to a Relater if you notice slower-than-average speech patterns; more moments of listening than of speaking; and references to actual, real-life experiences regarding either products or mutual acquaintances.

Relaters tend to express themselves tentatively in both their face-to-face and telephone conversations. They may say, "I'll need to consult Dr. Adams before I can make that decision," or "I'm not sure we can do that; I'll get back to you when I find out." As in other aspects of their lives, they often defer to the more human, proven way things have always been done. They typically feel more comfortable making decisions by conferring with others rather than by themselves. "What do you think?" and "How do you feel?" are common questions that people of this type may ask.

Clues From Letters

In written correspondence, Relaters may send letters just to keep in touch or to let you know they are thinking of you. Of the four personality types, this one is most likely to send thank-you notes for almost anything. Relaters are likely to organize their letters like they do their task lists—probably in sequential in-out order. Because they tend to write in a slower, more methodical manner, their work usually follows a systematic outline pattern.

The Thinker at the Office

Thinkers often carry their organizational tendencies into their work environments. Environmental clues include neat, highly organized desks with cleared tops so that they can work unimpeded by clutter. Their offices are clean, orderly, and professional, with everything in its appropriate place.

Notice the Walls

Charts, graphs, exhibits, models, credentials, and job-related pictures are often placed neatly on their office walls or shelves. Thinkers favor functional decor that enables them to work more efficiently. They tend to keep objects within reach, readily available when needed.

Where appropriate, you may notice state-of-the-art technology to further enhance efficiency.

Observable Characteristics

As people of few words, Thinkers tend to ask pertinent questions rather than to make statements. They typically speak more carefully and with less expression than the other types. Because they are reluctant to reveal personal feelings, they often use thinking words as opposed to feeling words.

Thinkers are non-contact people who prefer the formality of distance. This preference is reflected in the functional but uninviting arrangement of their desks and chairs, usually with the desks physically separating them from visitors. They generally are not fond of hugs and touches and prefer cool handshakes or brief telephone calls. When Thinkers walk, they usually move slowly and methodically toward a known destination.

Thinkers tend to wear conservative clothes, but ones with unique, often perfectly matched accessories. Although Socializers may draw attention to themselves with glitz and glitter, Thinkers usually prefer more understated, faultlessly groomed looks with not a hair out of place. But their tastes may differ from those of the people around them.

Thinkers like expressions of individuality and creativity, but within guidelines. Male Thinkers with beards seem to prefer short, well-manicured ones; if they smoke, they often prefer pipes—perhaps, someone noted, because taking a puff from a pipe allows them more time to think before answering questions. Because they prefer to explore life's complexities, they also may enjoy the intricacies of a specific kind of music or individual musical piece, whether jazz, classical, rock, etc. They drive well-built, practical cars that perform well, often in conservative and understated, but less common colors.

Observable Characteristics of a Thinker		
Verbal	**Vocal**	**Visual**
Orients to facts and tasks	Speaks with little inflection	Uses few facial expressions
Limits sharing of feelings	Uses few pitch variations	Tends to be non-contact oriented
Tends to be formal and proper	Uses less variety in vocal quality	Gestures infrequently
Focuses communication	Delivers words in a steady monotone	Moves deliberately
Uses less verbal, more written communication	Has low-volume, slower speech	Uses slow-moving body language

Telephone Clues

Formal greetings are one tipoff that you may be dealing with a Thinker. Time-conscious individuals of this type often get to a task just when they say they will. Many Thinkers call themselves by their given names, not by nicknames. Of course, there are exceptions.

They prefer brief, to-the-point telephone calls. Although they may not tell you, call them "Mr." or "Ms." or "Dr." Thinkers sometimes view jumping into a first-name basis as invasion of privacy, and they deal with others on a more formal basis. They typically retain their ground in stressful situations when they can maintain their position with concrete facts or reverse-control questions. They do this quietly and independently, first by avoiding others. Then they take on the problem in an orderly way that is aligned with their own plans.

Thinkers are inclined to talk in structured, careful speech patterns, almost weighing their words as they say them. They tend to ask pertinent questions and talk in quiet, observant, or cautious ways. Additionally, they may not volunteer much about their personal lives. They prefer to keep relationships formal, yet pleasant and businesslike. Less can be more to a Thinker—less conversation, self-disclosure, and verbal communication add up to a bigger comfort zone. Learn to hear between the lines: Longer than average silences, especially when asked more private questions, may signal annoyance or reluctance. When this occurs, ask, "Am I getting too personal?" Or ask, "If I'm asking uncomfortable questions, how could you let me know so I don't make a problem for either of us?" Thinkers may relax more if they think they have a way out.

Like Relaters, Thinkers tend to express themselves tentatively. "I'll check on that and let you know tomorrow." Or they may want to provide you with information so you can form your own conclusions. "I have a copy of that report in my files. If I send it to you, perhaps you can find what you're looking for." Both these approaches satisfy Thinkers' need for caution and correctness. They simply may not want to get misquoted or, possibly, involved in the first place.

Clues From Letters

Thinkers typically send letters to clarify or explain positions. Consequently, these letters may become rather long and filled with data. On the other hand, they may also be somewhat reserved or vague. Sometimes their letters are short, with enclosures or references to specific information. Whether they prefer the long or short form, Thinkers usually concentrate on processing data. They like to cover their bases so they are not misinterpreted.

Like Directors, in the interest of time, Thinkers may sign personal cards with just their names or with individual mottos, such as "In the spirit of growth, A.J. Williams." Even if you know them well, people of this type may include their surnames just so that there is no mistake about who sent this card.

If the Shoe Fits

The dimensions that determine type—Direct/Indirect and Self-Contained/Open—have their own innate strengths and weaknesses. In fact, many strengths, taken to extremes, can become weaknesses. The Direct/Self-Contained type can become overbearing when he or she pushes persistence too hard. Similarly, the Direct/Open type may turn manipulative; the Indirect/Open type, indecisive; or the Indirect/Self-Contained type, unreachable. These and other positive or negative characteristics shade the actions of all four types. Individuals representing all four may have the same assignment, but use different approaches. If a monthly report is due, one type may keep a day-by-day journal (Indirect/Self-Contained), another type may delegate the work (Direct/

Self-Contained), another may prefer completing it with a coworker (Indirect/Open), and yet another may prefer to stay up all night to complete it at the last minute (Direct/Open).

By now, you know how to recognize the four core types by observing environmental clues and external behaviors. The four combinations we've just discussed—Direct/Self-Contained, or Director; Direct/Open, or Socializer; Indirect/Open, or Relater; and Indirect/Self-Contained, or Thinker—all behave differently from one another in various situations. Whether at home, work, or at a social activity, they all naturally act true to their own types in an attempt to fill their needs and expectations. By acting themselves, they show their true core behavioral colors.

In the next chapter, Adaptability, you will read about getting along with all the behavioral types in their natural, and less natural, life environments. Chapter 6 suggests practical ways to enhance your adaptability so that you can have more productive relationships with people of all types. After that, you'll read about applying these concepts in the workplace (Chapter 7), leading and being led by each type (Chapter 8), and selling to and being sold by them (Chapter 9). Finally, the last chapter sums up the principles that this book set out to present. So read on to discover more about your relationship potential in different work environments.

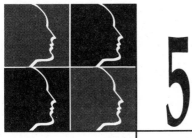

5

Creating Personal Power Through Behavioral Adaptability

What Is Behavioral Adaptability?

Behavioral adaptability is the key to success with the different types. With adaptability, we can treat other people the way they want to be treated. Behavioral adaptability is "the willingness and ability to behave in ways that are not necessarily characteristic of your style in order to deal effectively with the requirements of a situation or relationship." It is something applied more to yourself (to your own patterns, attitudes, and habits) than to others. It involves making strategic adjustments to how you communicate and behave, based on the needs of a relationship at a particular time. Adaptable people try to meet the expectations of others by practicing tact. They make the choice to go beyond their own comfort zones so others feel more comfortable.

What Adaptability Is Not

Adaptability does not mean imitating another person's behavioral style. It does mean adjusting your Openness, Self-Containedness, Directness, and Indirectness to be more in line with the other person's preferences. At the same time, it means maintaining your own identity and good sense. You *modify* your spots.

Does that mean that Thinkers prefer the company of Thinkers and that the other behavioral types prefer people who share their types? Yes and no. Two clichés apply. "Birds of a feather flock together" and "Opposites attract." Directors may admire other Directors' accomplishments and successes, but prefer to be more guarded with them at work to maintain their own power and authority.

Thinkers may appreciate Socializers for their joys of life, but avoid them at work because of their imprecision. Socializers may enjoy Thinkers for their command of the subject, but may stay aloof at work because of the Thinkers' perfectionism. Relaters and Directors may also admire one another's qualities or feel alienated by them. So what is a person to do?

Which Style Is Most Adaptable?

Remember that the willingness to try behaviors not necessarily characteristic of your own type is behavioral adaptability. It is different from your behavioral type. Your adaptability level affects the way other people perceive you. When you raise your adaptability level, you will discover that your trust and credibility go up; lower it, and they go down. Behavioral adaptability means adjusting your behavior to allow others to be more at ease, encouraged, and successful in your relationship.

No one style is naturally more adaptable than another. For a given situation, how people of each type make strategic adjustments varies. The decision to employ specific techniques of behavioral adaptability is made on a case-by-case basis. You can choose to be adaptable with one person and not with another. You can also choose to be quite adaptable with a person today and less so with that same person tomorrow. Behavioral adaptability concerns the way you manage your own communication and behaviors. It also involves how you manage the requirements that exist for a task or situation—whether other people are involved or not.

For example, when a Socializer works directly with a Thinker, the Socializer can practice behavioral adaptability by talking less, listening more, and focusing on the critical facts. Behavioral adaptability means adjusting your own behavior to make other people feel more at ease with you and the situation. You practice adaptability every time you slow down for a Thinker or Relater—or when you move a bit faster for a Socializer or a Director. Adaptability occurs when the Director or the Thinker takes the time to listen to a human-interest or family story told by a Socializer or a Relater.

The Adaptability Recipe

Adaptability is a phenomenon that has many characteristics. Formal research studies identified at least ten attributes of people who are highly adaptable and ten attributes of those who are less adaptable—a total of twenty traits in all. Of course, no person is likely to be either totally adaptable or nonadaptable. Instead, each of us possesses:

- Different general, overall levels of adaptability ranging from higher to lower

- Personal differences in various situations regarding levels of the two basic ingredients of adaptability—flexibility and versatility

- Specific key strengths and possible growth areas in the twenty behaviors that constitute adaptability potential

High and Low Adapters

Research conducted on adaptability has shown that most people view themselves as both more flexible and versatile than they are. In part, this is because people aspire toward who and what they want to be. As a result, their views of themselves include both how they intend to act and how they actually do act. However, the reality of observable behavior is based only on the second element.

Another factor that explains this gap in the idealized versus actual level of adaptability is that it is not easy to be adaptable. Most people are not even aware of the ten behaviors that allow them to achieve their potential, let alone developed these behaviors as personal strengths. Similarly, most people have not thought about the ten other behaviors that undermine their potential strengths. Following are all twenty behaviors, divided into ten flexibility strengths and weaknesses and ten versatility plus and minus points.

Higher flexibility is characterized by these personal attitudes:

- **Confidence**—belief in yourself, trusting your own judgment and resourcefulness

- **Tolerance**—open-minded acceptance; willingness to defer judgment because of limited time or information

- **Empathy**—sensitivity to another's point of view; caring approach toward others (without being overwhelmed or manipulated by people)

- **Positiveness**—maintaining a state of positive expectations about people and situations, including a positive state of energy in your thoughts and emotional patterns

- **Respect for others**—a desire to understand, accept, and consider mutual and separate interests, choices, and commitments

Lower flexibility is characterized by the following personal attitudes:

- **Rigidity**—holding the attitude of "my way or not at all"

- **Competition with others**—allowing your need to compete to interfere with the best possible outcome for everyone

- **Discontent**—never being positive or completely happy about anything

- **Being unapproachable**—making it known that you do not want people around you

- **Difficulty in dealing with ambiguity**—seeing situations as "either/or"; needing closure on one meaning, one interpretation, or one outcome

If you list the successful individuals you admire, you probably will notice your list is full of people with high flexibility strengths. Those with lower flexibility characteristics seldom seem to make the list.

The other half of this adaptability formula is versatility. Research indicates that people have a more clear-cut understanding of and a higher developed level of flexibility than versatility. Versatility, instead, involves a set of personal *aptitudes*, which are distinctly different from merely being willing to adapt. Many people are willing to modify their behaviors but simply lack the required abilities. Versatility is a complex set of mental and emotional abilities that people acquire over time; these abilities come through a variety of sources, such as formal education, daily life experiences, and observations of others who display these same behaviors.

The good news is that versatility can be learned. People are not born either high or low in versatility. But more versatile people tend to approach every situation as a new opportunity for learning and growing. And, of course, others make the opposite decision and get the consequences that go along with the easier way of doing things in life.

Higher versatility is characterized by these personal aptitudes:

- **Resilience**—learning how to cope in spite of setbacks, barriers, or limited resources

- **Vision**—foresight, creativity, and imagination

- **Attentiveness**—being mindful and aware of stimuli in the environment; focused on reality

- **Competence**—the capability to manage required tasks and be knowledgeable about required subjects and people, including uses and updates of appropriate abilities

- **Self-correction**—the ability to initiate and evaluate oneself, seeking feedback as appropriate, with a problem-solving mind-set and approach to matters

Lower versatility is characterized by the following personal aptitudes:

- **Subjectiveness**—seeing everything from your own perspective

- **Bluntness**—being assertive about personal opinions and beliefs without taking other people's feelings into account

- **Resistance**—balking at suggestions that you do not like

- **Single-mindedness**—tunnel vision or narrow-mindedness

- **Unreasonable risk-taking**—overemphasizing the resources that you have or can acquire to accomplish your objectives

Everyone Can Become More Adaptable

The good news is that you can, in fact, become more adaptable. The accompanying bad news is that adaptability does not happen overnight, by wishing for it, or without occasional regressions back to old, comfortable behaviors. Adaptability involves learning techniques of mind over matter; therefore, you can speed up the process and increase your probability for success by focusing on who you are. Coming full circle, this means dealing with who you are. It also means making a personal commitment to work toward overcoming the easier, more natural behaviors you will occasionally slip back into.

You can teach yourself to stay on the road to adaptability when you fall back into your old habits. The "Road

Map to Personal Adaptability" will help you to increase your own flexibility and versatility. You can also use it to coach and help your friends, family, coworkers, and others through the same learning process. Again, this process begins with who you are. From there, you can work on either those appropriate *attitude* changes or *aptitude* changes to develop the potentials related to your own unique behavioral tendencies.

Here's how to use your own road map. First identify your strongest behavioral tendency (Director, Socializer, Relater, or Thinker). Select just one goal, either flexibility or versatility, but not both at once. Then look across the appropriate row and under the corresponding column to find what you can do to further develop your skills.

Because people do not behave in a vacuum, you can refine these general self-adaptations, depending on the types of individuals with whom you interact. Here, then, is a brief list of specific types of adaptations to use when you interact with each of the four types. These basic action strategies for increasing flexibility and versatility are good starting points for increasing your own effectiveness. But based on the natural human condition, they tend to be ongoing challenges. Therefore, a second approach that complements this lifelong road map focuses on one of the many adaptability strengths noted previously.

Creating Personal Power

A wise person once commented, "A little knowledge can be a dangerous thing." In the field of formal education, this quotation is sometimes called the sophomoric syndrome. That is, as people begin to learn about a new topic,

✦ Road Map to Personal Adaptability ✦

If you are a...	How to Increase Flexibility	How to Increase Versatility
	Lower your overemphasis on...	*Develop and demonstrate more...*
Director	Control of other people and conditions	Supportive skills and actions Examples: listening, open-ended questions, positive reinforcement of others
Socializer	Approval from other people or groups as the primary determinants of appropriate choices for you	Directive skills and actions Examples: self-assertion, conflict resolution, negotiations
Relater	Resistance to new opportunities; limiting your options by undue demand for or dependence on stability or risk-free choices	Directive skills and actions Examples: negotiation, divergent thinking
Thinker	Unnecessary perfectionism and the tendency to focus on weaknesses (rather than strengths) and faults in oneself and others	Supportive skills and actions Examples: empathic listening, positive reinforcement of others, involvement with others with complementary strengths

they tend to jump to oversimplified and incomplete conclusions. When that happens, they are often less successful than they might be otherwise. But with continuing
effort, thought, and increased study, they eventually
graduate to a higher level of excellence. In terms of
adaptability, it is essential to understand the following
principles:

1. Adaptability is not a goal by itself, but a means to
   the end of increased personal effectiveness and
   success.

2. A key to effectiveness is to realize what level and
   type of adaptability component(s) are the critical
   factors in achieving a targeted goal.

   Examples:

   "The key to getting this sale is to be a lot more
   flexible than I am naturally with this type of
   strong-willed person."

   "If I don't lower my already high tendency to be
   too flexible and accommodating, I'm likely to continue giving away the store. Conditions have
   changed and I can't afford to do that any longer
   because it conflicts with the results I want."

3. Being adaptable also means assessing other resources that can allow you to get your desired
   outcomes by acting smarter.

   Example:

   Although you have developed the competencies
   required to successfully complete a known task,
   you work with three other people who also pos-
   sess these same talents. However, they do not
   have the same pressing, competing priorities fac-

⊕ **Action Plan** ⊕

When you deal with...	Take these actions:
Directors	Get right to the point quickly and decisively without getting bogged down in minute details. Operate with conviction, know what you are doing, and do not try to bluff.
Socializers	Show your energy and liveliness while focusing on the give-and-take interaction. Make your encounter fun, upbeat, and enjoyable!
Relaters	Cultivate a casual, easy-going, personable, one-on-one relationship. Treat them with warmth, feeling, and sensitivity.
Thinkers	Use an orderly, logical, accurate approach that focuses on the process and procedures. Give them well-thought, accurate documentation.

ing them as you do. In this case, adaptability includes having the vision and self-corrective aptitudes to seek one or more available resources to help you to manage your situation appropriately.

Isn't that better than trying to be superhuman and doing it all yourself?

4. Adaptability, then, is important because it directly relates to your degree of achieved success in a variety of life's opportunities. These range from relationships with other people to coping with changing conditions around you to managing different types of situations.

Extreme Behaviors

At times people may perceive extreme adaptability as acting indecisive, walking a fence, or acting two-faced. A person who maintains high adaptability in all situations may not be able to avoid personal stress and ultimate inefficiency. Tension also develops from the strain of behaving in an unfamiliar manner with others. This tension is usually temporary and may be worth experiencing if you gain rapport with the other person.

The other extreme of the continuum is no behavioral adaptability. Others view this person as rigid and uncompromising because of an insistence on behaving at his or her own pace and priority.

Adaptability is important to successful relationships of all kinds. People often adopt at least a partially different role in their professional lives than they do in their social and personal lives. This adaptation is made to manage the professional requirements of their jobs more successfully. Interestingly, many people tend to be more adaptable at work with people they do not know well than they are at home with people they know better. Why? People generally want to create a good impression at work; at home, they may relax and act themselves to the point of unintentionally stepping on other family members' toes. Although this may not be an attractive family portrait, it is often an accurate one.

To better understand how adaptability affects the management of various situations, look at its application to a variety of professions and their related job requirements. This process is essentially the same one that is used by major selection, recruiting, and career development consulting firms around the world.

You can profile any role or job in terms of adaptability. This is not to say that a person's behavioral style is not important as well. However, once selected for a job, a person's level of flexibility and versatility determines whether he or she will be a higher performer or a lower performer.

Let's take a deeper look at this idea as it relates to other types of position requirements. A sales job that involves a single, simple product line is likely to require high flexibility, but may not require much versatility. Another sales job involving multiple products that are complex and changing usually requires both high flexibility and high versatility. Contrast this with the position of nuclear researcher, which requires very high versatility but much lower flexibility. This lower flexibility protects this person and others from being open to trying possibilities that may literally explode in their faces. Finally, picture the job requirements of a single working parent of two teenagers. Here again, versatility is the key ingredient in managing the myriad competing expectations and demands. Of course, a moderate level of flexibility allows peace and order to prevail!

Adaptability Works

Effectively adaptable people meet the key expectations of others in specific situations—whether in personal or business relationships. Through attention and practice, you can manage your adaptability strategically by recognizing when a modest compromise is appropriate. You also will understand when it is necessary to adapt to the other person's behavioral style.

Practice managing relationships in a way that allows everyone to win. Be tactful, reasonable, understanding, comfortable to talk to, and nonjudgmental. These actions result in a moderate position between the two extremes. You probably can meet the needs of the other person as well as your own. Adapt your pace and your priorities. Work at relationships so that everybody wins—at work, with friends, and with family.

Knowing the degree to which you are Direct/Indirect and Open/Self-Contained helps you to deal better with yourself and others. Just as you discovered your own unique behavioral type and its characteristics, you can learn to identify others' key strengths and weaknesses. Recognizing sterling traits and potential pitfalls of diverse people means you can better understand their behaviors and relate to them more effectively.

When you make efforts to accommodate another person's expectations and tendencies, you automatically decrease tension and increase trust. Adaptability enables you to interact more productively, helps you in strained situations, and assists you in establishing rapport and credibility. It can make the difference between a productive and an ineffective interpersonal relationship. Your adaptability level also influences how others judge their relationships with you. Raise your adaptability level, and trust and credibility soar; lower your adaptability level, and trust and credibility plummet.

Another way of looking at this whole matter is from the perspective of maturity. Mature people know themselves. They understand basic behavioral types and freely express their core patterns. However, when problems or opportunities arise, they readily and deliberately adjust their core patterns to meet these needs. Immature people, on the other hand, lose effectiveness in dealing with the real world when they lock into their own styles. By disregarding the needs of others, they end up causing conflict and tension, leading to less satisfaction and fulfillment in their life environments.

There are four key rewards that make our efforts at becoming more mature and adaptable worthwhile. These benefits define the characteristics of people who are the higher performers in life. By reading, reflecting, and then taking the guided actions suggested in this book, you too can achieve this level of excellence in your own life. Do you want to become more:

- Successful?

- Effective?

- Satisfied?

- Fulfilled?

If so, you can get started today based on what you learned in these first five chapters. Now read the remaining chapters for even more powerful insights about how you can become all that you can truly be.

6

Improving Flexibility and Versatility

Flexibility

The flexibility dimension of adaptability involves your personal attitudes toward yourself, others, and the situations you face. It reflects your willingness quotient for changing your perspective and/or your position when appropriate. The five positive traits that capture the essence of your flexibility potential are confidence, tolerance, empathy, positiveness, and respect for others.

Confidence

Having confidence means that you believe in yourself and you trust your own judgment and resourcefulness. In his many books on self-esteem, Dr. Nathaniel Branden defines self-esteem as the sum of self-confidence and self-respect. Self-confidence is believing that you can function reasonably well in the world. People reported by others to have high confidence also generate this sense of credibility and trustworthiness in other people through their proactive, optimistic, forward-moving approach.

You feel confident when making choices that satisfy your own needs and enable you to chart your life's course. Having confidence in a variety of situations, such as in gaining influence with someone or handling work loads, would flow from a general self-confidence about your proven experience of successfully meeting life's challenges. Self-confidence can be built by recording successes and then affirming the inner strengths that contributed to it. Finally, it is important to note those

newer, emerging strengths and their contribution to continuing self-empowerment.

Tolerance

Tolerance means being open to opinions and practices
that are different from your own. An early start on tolerance for differences is a great gift for parents to give to
children. Some of us have to learn to become more toler-
ant in a world characterized by the factual reality of
human differences; most of us could benefit from becoming more adept at it. One simple tip for building this
quality is to realize that others' views and practices are
just that. It does not mean that these must become ours.
And yet they may provide new insights or options for
realistically dealing with the realities of other people—not
just our own.

Empathy

The root of the word empathy is pathos, the Greek word
for feeling. Sympathy means acknowledging the feelings
of someone else, but empathy says, "I understand how
you feel. I can put myself in your shoes." Sympathy
results in kindness and sometimes pity. Empathy results
in actually recognizing the feelings of the other person
without taking responsibility for them.

Empathy is much easier to feel when you care about
the other person and take the time to feel the way that he
or she feels. In the worlds of business, politics, or the
professions, a feeling of empathy may not come as easily.
Putting empathy into practical action involves dealing
with our emotions, concerns, or fears. It involves facilitat-

ing the rebirth of positive thoughts and feelings through tender encouragement given to people when they need it.

Positiveness

Positiveness means maintaining a state of optimistic expectations about people and situations, including a proactive, forward-looking and moving state of energy and action. It comes from deep within our spirits. Positiveness is built on having an appreciation of life, on knowing our strengths, and on surrounding ourselves with others who genuinely care about our well-being.

Your personal philosophy acknowledges who you are and your purpose for being alive. A truly positive philosophy encompasses more than just "me." It also involves positive attitudes toward others—regardless of differences.

The second aspect of positiveness comes from knowing those strengths you have to build on to achieve your goals and purpose. This can be developed by taking a personal inventory of your talents, interests, and aspirations and then taking repeated action that gets the positive results that provide purpose in your life.

However, having a positive personal philosophy and action plan will only get you so far. A third key aspect of positiveness is strengthening yourself through other sources of the same or complementary energy. Supportive relationships provide a positive recharge when our own resources run low; they help focus on our inherent strengths to recover from the setbacks and adversities encountered in life.

Respect for Others

The fifth essential flexibility characteristic is respect for others. When we treat people as we seek to be treated, it may cause tension—because the other person may not like our way. Instead, if we treat others the way they want to be treated, we capture the true spirit and actual intention of the Golden Rule. We now are considering and responding to the other person. Respecting others means learning to treat people differently, according to their needs and beliefs, not ours. This can lead to greater moral understanding and acceptance among individuals and groups. For many people and cultures, this quality is demonstrated as personal integrity.

"Respect for others" can be narrowly interpreted as "live and let live," or more comprehensively as seeking common, shared interests and then working together to reach win-win results. This attitude breaks down the "us and them" mentality and leads to a perspective that focuses on the "us" opportunities in life. Two methods for developing this attitude are (1) practicing the spirit of the Golden Rule, and (2) using a win-win problem-solving approach with people.

Developing and demonstrating the five positive elements of high flexibility puts people in the position of being willing to adapt their behavior to meet both the needs of others and themselves. But being willing to adapt is only half of the story. The second half of the power to adapt comes from demonstrating the actual ability to adapt—"versatility."

Versatility

The good news is that versatility, like flexibility, can be developed. More versatile people tend to approach situations as new opportunities for continuous learning and improvement. Each individual can choose whether or not to become more versatile. The five essential versatility traits are resilience, vision, attentiveness, competence, and self-correction.

Resilience

In terms of versatility, resilience means coping in spite of setbacks, barriers, or limited resources. It is a measure of hardiness and perseverance. Resilient people overcome obstacles. Resilience has to do with emotional strength and mental toughness.

The trait of resilience involves behaviors that lead to eventual success through persistent effort. Although it is related to the flexibility traits of self-confidence and a positive attitude, resilience is qualitatively different in terms of the driving approach of the resilient person. History is filled with repeated heroic examples of such "never-give-up" individuals—some of whom were more positive and self-confident than others. Resilience is developed by dealing with situations that are outside our comfort zones—ones that call for acquiring and applying new knowledge, skills, and attitudes. It is a personal continuous improvement behavior pattern.

Vision

Someone who has vision can see desired outcomes for the future and how to reach them. Vision provides a common focus for energizing people toward an agreed-on purpose and goals as well as action strategies for getting there. With the rate, nature, and direction of change today, it is even more necessary to envision future possible scenarios. Without such a vision, people often get lost in the trivia of daily life or feel empty and purposeless about their own activities and continuing focus.

Visions take a variety of forms, such as to make more money, to end a problem, to improve a situation, to create or innovate, or to have more fun. Some people have this visionary talent while others see only problems or present demands. Visioning can be developed by techniques such as imagining the future five to ten years from now and visualizing where you or your company would like to be. With this information, you then assess the gap between where you are now and where you would like to be and chart a course to close the gap.

Attentiveness

Attentiveness means being aware of what is going on in your environment. It can be as simple as noticing when someone is getting bored and sensing that now is not the right time to put your ideas across. Attentive people also know when to act and when not to act; they notice trends, patterns, variations, and opportunities.

Attentiveness is also the ability to focus on a problem and to identify its essential components. It involves being open to outside stimuli. Attentive people are open to information coming in through various channels or modalities—seeing, hearing, touching, smelling, and so on.

Being attentive requires emptying ourselves of other thoughts and set ways of seeing things. When we use our senses to absorb all that we can about a situation or person, we can adjust our behavior more accurately. Attentive people can exercise the power of vision to make positive changes for themselves and others. Attentiveness is really a function of personal effort and continually building increasing levels of consciousness.

Competence

Competence, as used here, goes beyond having specific expertise in selected areas. Although it certainly does mean being knowledgeable and skillful in your field of work or interest, competence also means having a problem-solving capability that allows you to go beyond your own specialties; it allows you to quickly and adeptly develop and demonstrate a working knowledge of new or different subjects, people, and situations. Therefore, competent adaptiveness involves both task- and people-directed actions.

Exhibiting competence involves knowing what you are doing, knowing how to get something done, and then communicating effectively with others. On an obvious level, competence has to do with being able to do what you say you can do. But competence has other dimensions. Research on high achievers gives keen insights about personal competence. Such individuals continuously set realistic personal goals, address the resources and barriers likely to affect progress, and then take actions continuously along the way that contribute to success. Periodically, they also take time out to reflect on those key actions, attitudes, and factors that point toward continuing success.

Self-Correction

The fifth and final versatility trait is self-correction. This is the ability to initiate change, evaluate the results, and make ongoing corrections that lead to continuing improvement. Such people seek feedback as food for further thought and as free gifts for solving problems. They are driven more toward being better than being right. Individuals with this strength know when they have displayed nonproductive behavior patterns.

Self-correction is focused on the drive for excellence and personal quality. When things are going well, people generally do not think about changing anything. Only when something is new, incomplete, or imperfect do they see the opportunity to make corrections. This is where practices like mentoring, feedback, goal setting, and continuous improvement are so valuable.

Self-correction allows us to make course corrections by learning from our mistakes. It also allows us to get better at spotting and capitalizing on opportunities for change before situations deteriorate or before minor difficulties become major problems. One simple technique for self-correction is a "daily review." At the end of each day, take five minutes to log in a personal journal the progress made toward specific self-correction objectives and any key actions required the next day to continue or strengthen this progress.

Conclusion

Adaptation requires both flexibility and versatility. Flexibility is a willingness to adapt behavior, and it is enhanced by confidence, tolerance, empathy, positiveness, and respect for others. Versatility is the actual ability to adapt behavior, which is built on the traits of resilience, vision, attentiveness, competence, and self-correction.

The flexibility dimension of adaptability involves personal attitudes toward oneself, others, and situations. It indicates a person's degree of willingness to change perspective or position when appropriate. Higher flexibility attitudes tend to indicate that a person has a higher level of security and a sense of personal worth or well-being. They also suggest an open-minded, searching attitude in dealing with people and situations and positive expectations about one's own goals and desired results, as well as those of others.

In comparison to flexible individuals, highly versatile people have distinctive abilities to manage a variety of situations realistically and productively, as well as the stresses that accompany them. In addition, their actions are clearly goal oriented; these actions serve a meaningful purpose in their personal aspirations, in their relationships with others, and in the outcomes they want. Versatile people also exhibit problem-solving actions that match the requirements of different situations.

You do not have to be a prisoner of your own behavioral tendencies and patterns. Instead, by increasing your personal flexibility and versatility, you can gain personal success and effectiveness by managing yourself, your relationships, and the situations you encounter. You yourself are in charge of whether you choose to be a person with higher or lower flexibility and versatility.

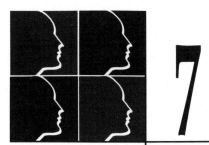

7

On the Job:
Problem Solving
in the Workplace

Behavioral Types at Work

As you read this chapter, think of specific individuals you know at work who represent each of the four behavioral styles—Director, Socializer, Relater, and Thinker. How can you apply what you have learned to improve your working relationships with each one? What are some characteristics that work to the advantage of these people in their job performance? Which characteristics work against them?

To understand the connections between behavioral type and daily work performance, it is important to realize how these four tendencies affect your work. All jobs involve different types of problem-solving tasks. And, because job requirements differ, so does the degree of natural match or fit with your preferred behavior pattern. More complex jobs call for increased adaptability to fulfill job expectations that may be quite different from your own sources of natural inner motivation.

Director Behavior in a Work Setting

Directors prefer power positions and career areas in which they can take charge, such as the following:

- President or CEO (i.e., the formally recognized leader)
- Politician
- Police or military officer
- Executive or manager

- Entrepreneur

- Owner of a company

- General contractor

How Directors Think

Typical Directors see themselves as problem-oriented managers who enjoy challenges just because the challenges exist. They like the opportunity to complete tasks creatively—their own way, of course. Directors are independent, strong willed, restless, and goal oriented. Other people tend to view them as highly confident, although this may not be true. However, when Directors read an article that they don't understand, they may instinctively react as if the article is flawed. Their self-images are high, and so is their output.

How Directors Work

Because of their drive for specific and concrete results, Directors often put in extra hours at the office. At the extreme, their high results orientation can manifest in an overextended work pattern. When this happens, they pay a high price for their success—their personal and social lives may fall apart from neglect while their work-related attainments accumulate.

When Directors perceive that others are not producing enough, they may react with a message designed to stimulate others to action: "Don't just stand there. Do something!" Directors typically show administrative and leadership qualities that reflect their ability to initiate and to accomplish tasks, and then to juggle them.

Directors can pick up three balls (tasks) and keep them all in the air at the same time. They're multiphasic behavior specialists who can do many things well simultaneously. After adapting to juggling three balls, they pick up another and another. They end up juggling all of them faster than the eye can see. However, the pressure mounts as they try to maximize the quantity of tasks or the quality of results.

Logically, it makes sense to drop one ball to relieve some pressure. However, for Directors to admit that they cannot do it all tarnishes their images. They like impressing others with their work loads until they get bored or tired of not-enough-hours-in-the-day balancing acts. Then they tend to drop everything and take up new directions for their activities until they tire of the same patterns again. Directors typically call this "reordering priorities."

Directors can help themselves by learning when to walk away from a project and let others assume control. If this does not happen, Directors' tendencies to hold on can frustrate others. People also tend to respond more favorably to Directors who verbalize the reasons for their conclusions and pace themselves to project more relaxed states. They can also soften their reprimands by tempering criticism with healthy doses of genuine praise.

What Motivates Directors

Adult Directors often like to accumulate items—especially ones they think will save time or money. Efficiency is the name of the game. One Director told us that he is so impatient that he never buys green tomatoes. Another relishes the fast-forward feature on the VCR that lets her bypass TV commercials. A third person uses a car phone to make maximum use of driving time; she can't wait to get others to carry out her ideas. Yet another Director tells his secretary to fax his mail to him when he is away from the office.

Because Directors are so competitive, they may view themselves as participating in perpetual contests with others. Other styles may see themselves as merely giving reports—period. This is not true for Directors. Their reports compete for position against those of others. They need to have control, so one-upmanship can become a favorite game. In this extreme, Directors fill the role of the all-seeing, all-knowing expert. Everyone else, by contrast, becomes insignificant.

Despite their strong images, Directors also have their own unique limitations. They are selective listeners who tend to tune out small talk. To increase adaptability, their listening skills and their awareness of others' needs require improvement. Instead of just telling others what to do, hearing their thoughts and opinions can help Directors to get things done more smoothly—for the good of everyone.

Consequently, Directors tend to work more favorably with complementary types who contribute stability, predictability, and support toward their common objectives. Each of these other types can help Directors to put tasks into perspective, recharge their batteries, or bolster temporarily bruised egos. Other people's feedback can also help Directors to stay on track with objectivity, accuracy, and responsiveness to others' needs.

How to Approach Directors

Sometimes others may interpret Directors' hustle and impatience as "Don't interrupt." Ironically, when this happens, Directors may sabotage the very control they want. If coworkers and employees perceive a Director as overloaded with too much work, they may hesitate to disturb that person or cause delays. Therefore, that Director may know less about what is happening than he or she would by being more accessible.

Directors tend not to feel as bound by conventional practices as the other types. They prefer to answer to the higher authority of themselves; people of this type want to be their own bosses so they can have control over the results they want. To satisfy their need for results, Directors seek or create opportunities for change. They gravitate toward high-risk situations because the excitement of challenges fuels their actions.

Some Directors naturally combine pleasure with business. Consider the following example of Director Dan, who decided to give his employees a special surprise for Christmas—a combined business/pleasure trip to Honolulu.

> From bus excursions to daily seminars and discussion groups, Dan arranged the complete itinerary. He thought his staff would eagerly embrace his plans, but was extremely disappointed to overhear a few of them complaining about the fixed agenda:
>
> "Who does he think he is? Giving us a supposed vacation and bouncing us around in workshops and seminars, not to mention spending every breathing minute with him!"

"Yes, I know what you mean. Just once, I wish he'd ask us what we want instead of doing what he wants."

"Here, here!"

When he heard this, Dan's first impulse was to rush in and tell those ingrates a thing or three; however, he waited and decided to call his wife, Jean, to tell her what happened.

"I can understand their point, Dan. It sounds as though they just want to participate in the decision making instead of being told what to do."

"Hmmm. I guess my way might seem a bit autocratic."

"I'm glad you see it that way, Dan."

"Maybe I'll call an informal meeting so they can let me know just what they want."

So he did. The employees thanked him, but also told him they'd like a few days just to be with their families without having to check in with anyone but themselves.

"Is that all?" Dan asked. The group agreed.

"This was a lot easier than I thought it would be," Dan observed.

Fortunately, Dan put himself in his employees' shoes and became willing to see their point of view—they wanted to be part of the decision. For Dan, it seemed much easier to make the decisions and then tell everybody else to follow through. But what he wanted and what they wanted didn't necessarily match.

Director Leaders

Directors are outspoken, no-nonsense, take-control types. Harry Truman summed up the Directors' work-style attitude with his now famous statement: "If you can't stand the heat, get out of the kitchen." Directors exhibit personal needs to lead decisively and to direct action for fast results. Under stress, Directors lash out and forcefully take charge in differing ways.

In extreme cases, Directors may, at times, have to live by the watchwords, "Ready! Fire! Aim!" This results from their natural tendencies to plunge in without much risk-assessing forethought.

A good example is that of an elementary school principal who chose to manage her school in typical Director fashion—her way. She decided arbitrarily to rescind the parents' privilege to request teachers for their children. Her rationale was that reading all those forms wasted her secretary's time. The parents had different ideas and became angry that they had not been consulted. The resulting furor could have been prevented if she had only stopped to ask, "What do you think?" In reality, this principal did not even have to do what the parents wanted, as long as she heard their ideas. The parents resented her dictatorial approach.

This principal, following her Director instincts, focused on the result, not the steps leading to it. To accomplish the desired end, she tried to shape the environment by overcoming the opposition. Unfortunately for her, she discovered the parents did not necessarily want their environment shaped, especially without their feedback.

Even benevolent dictators collide with their subjects when they try to rule by themselves.

Lee Iacocca, another Director, talks about how he learned to merge his temperament with other styles. His management philosophy, as described in his biography, *Iacocca*, is as follows: "In the end, all business operations can be reduced to three words: people, products, profits. People come first. Unless you have a good team, you can't do much with the other two." Iacocca, a living Director legend, illustrates the fact that collaborative team playing pays off for Directors and others!

Because Directors view themselves as chiefs, not just members of the team, they may resist deeper involvement in work teams. Stress, especially, brings out Directors' natural apprehension about people. Under duress, Directors may even seize control—a natural "me-first" tendency. Consequently, Directors need coworkers who draw them into the group. Directors often take themselves too seriously and can benefit from gentle reminders to take life less seriously and to laugh at themselves.

As natural doers, Directors may need some help channeling their energies; they may have trouble distinguishing the realistic from the awe inspiring. Of all the types, this one is the most likely to try even harder when told "That's impossible."

When Directors learn to become aware of other people's feelings, they become more successful in developing satisfying relationships with them. Because of their natural authoritarianism, Directors may need to work on when to consciously back off, slow down, and listen to other people's ideas and concerns. Besides bolstering their people skills, they can also attend to analyzing tasks

⊕ **Remember** ⊕

Directors' Business Characteristics

- Prefer time frames
- Seek personal control
- Get to the point
- Strive to feel important and be noteworthy in their jobs
- Demonstrate persistence and single-mindedness to reach goals
- Express high ego strength
- Prefer to downplay feelings and relationships
- Focus on task actions that lead to tangible outcomes
- Implement changes in the workplace
- Delegate duties freely in order to take on more projects

Directors' Preferred Business Situations

- Like to be in charge
- Like to tell others what to do
- Like challenging work loads that fuel their energy levels
- Oversee or know about employees' or coworkers' business activities
- Say what is on their minds without being concerned about hurting anybody's feelings
- Enjoy taking risks
- Enjoy being involved in changes
- Prefer to interpret the rules and answer to themselves alone
- Interested in the answers to "what" questions, not "how" questions
- Like to see a logical road toward increasing and ongoing advancement

more thoroughly. Directors instinctively want to hurry on to the next challenge. However, they can often ward off the problems that result from hastiness by searching out more details at the beginning.

Other behavioral types may not share Directors' preferences for quick results and blunt straightforwardness. By becoming less rigid in their direct approaches with others, Directors can better learn to manage the differences between themselves and others.

Socializer Behavior in a Work Setting

Socializers prefer careers that maximize their influence with people and in which they can socialize, mingle, and gain positive feedback, such as the following:

- Public-relations specialist
- Entertainer
- Professional host (talk show, party, restaurant, airline, etc.)
- Recreation director
- Politician
- Personnel interviewer
- Salesperson

How Socializers Think

Socializers think aloud. Desks confine them, so they typically stroll around the office talking to nearly everyone, from the custodian to the boss along the way, calling them by their first names. In the process, they seek others' reactions to almost anything and everything, but they visibly warm up to comments about themselves.

People with other styles may view this behavior as avoiding work. But appearances can be deceptive. While Socializers weave their way around the office, they bounce ideas off the people along the way. Socializers often do not merely talk—they brainstorm with virtually anyone they encounter. It is important for Socializers to find out how other people feel about their ideas. They like the feedback and the occasional compliments that these conversations provide. People of this type enjoy casual, relaxed environments in which they can allow their impulses free rein. Desk-hopping also satisfies their need for companionship. Socializers seek out people first to share the present, with one eye on future experiences with them. Talking with coworkers happily mixes business with pleasure for people of this type. Socializers like to play and mingle as they learn, earn, and do practically everything else.

As inductive thinkers, Socializers naturally think first about the big picture, then of details. After seeing the broad overview, they prefer not to dwell on specifics personally. Socializers are intuitive and may naturally come up with assorted ideas—some practical and some not. If the ideas feel right, Socializers will pitch those ideas to others to elicit their feedback and enthusiasm. This can also serve the purpose of pulling Socializers back to reality if they venture too far out.

How Socializers Work

Socializers like warmth, friendliness, and approval. Because they favor interacting with people on more than just a business level, they want to be friends before doing business. You probably are dealing with a Socializer if a client suggests meeting for lunch, a social drink, or dinner and asks questions like, "What exciting things are happening with you?"

Like Directors, Socializers share a quick pace. While Directors keep themselves busy with tasks, Socializers tend to move about the office in a flurry of activity. They even walk in a way that reflects optimism and energy. They observe as they go, avoiding obstacles and potential problems.

Because Socializers are naturally talkative and people oriented, they seek inclusion by others, popularity, social recognition, and (probably) freedom from too much detail. Jobs that fill these needs use their natural strengths. As with the other types, jobs do not equate to behavioral type; however, many Socializers gravitate toward people-oriented, high visibility professions that fill their innate needs.

Consider Disney employees. Disney hires vast numbers of Socializers who act just as peppy and people oriented at 10:00 P.M. as they did at 10:00 A.M. Tour guides still smile and carry on verbal repartee at the ends of their shifts. This characteristic cannot be taught; employees either become energized by mingling with people or they don't. Socializers do. Disney even provides people-free decompression areas for its employees during breaks so they can maintain their positive energy levels with guests.

Socializers want companionship and social recognition, so their contributions to group morale often satisfy these needs. At work, they like to know each person's first name and something about him or her. They can benefit from feedback from their coworkers, especially those who represent other behavioral types. Just as Relaters contribute stability, Thinkers seek accuracy, and Directors add decisiveness, Socializers give their enthusiasm and energy. Tactful reminders and help organizing and setting priorities can help the entire office to function more smoothly. Because Socializers tend to be open books, the other types can detect when they are having an off day and give them a boost with a compliment or two.

Socializers may have so many things going on that they may forget to finish tasks by their deadlines; other times they may procrastinate until the last minute because of their multiple priorities. Writing things down and setting priorities can help the Socializer remember when to do what.

What Motivates Socializers

At heart, Socializers are dreamers who are good at getting others caught up in their ideas. Their persuasive powers may amaze admirers and frustrate detractors simultaneously. Socializers show smooth-talking tendencies, which, at the extreme, appear to be either silver-tongued oration or evasive double-talk.

As true extroverts, Socializers typically look outside themselves to renew their energies. They enjoy motivational books, tapes, and speeches—pick-me-ups that recharge their batteries and help them to overcome obstacles. These avenues are seen as practical growth opportunities. Socializers even prefer the terms "opportunity" or "challenge" instead of "problem." Problems are too mired in negativism to fit comfortably with Socializers' optimistic outlooks.

Socializer Leaders

As leaders, Socializers like spontaneous, expressive actions for noticeable results. "Think positively," they may say, trying to encourage employees, peers, or superiors to function smoothly. Statements like "Follow that dream" and "Climb every mountain" sum up Socializer feelings. Though typically less motivated by change than Directors, Socializers become more susceptible to risk taking when pressured by others to take the chance. If they have not fully considered all of the ramifications, Socializers may regret their impulsiveness after it is too late.

How to Approach Socializers

Because Socializers like to talk a lot—to others and to themselves—they are likely to say inappropriate things more often than most of the other types. When talkativeness and emotionality mix, problems may set in. Learning when to stop talking and start listening can help Socializers grow. Sometimes their naturally impulsive behaviors energize us; at other times their spontaneity requires more restraint.

Socializers are idea people who throw ideas out. This impulsive habit can get them in trouble when others think a commitment has been made, but the Socializer sees the situation differently. Realistically, this type is much better at generating ideas than implementing them.

Socializers can pump up their flexibility by better containing their time and emotions and by developing more objective mind-sets. They can benefit by spending more time checking, verifying, specifying, and organizing, or getting someone else to do it for them. Otherwise,

⊕ **Remember** ⊕

Socializers' Business Characteristics

- Like to brainstorm
- Enjoy interactions with colleagues and others
- Want freedom from control, details, or complexity
- Like to influence or motivate others
- Like the feeling of being a key part of an exciting team
- Want to be included by others in important projects, activities, or events
- Get bored easily by routine and repetition
- May trust others without reservation
- Tend to listen to others without checking for themselves
- Have short attention spans and do well with many short breaks

Socializers' Preferred Business Situations

- Like to work participatively with others
- Need immediate feedback to get or stay on course
- Like to mingle with all levels of associates
- Call others by their first names
- Enjoy compliments about themselves
- Appreciate recognition of their accomplishments
- Seek stimulating environments that are friendly and favorable
- Are motivated to work toward known, specific, quickly attainable incentives
- Stay open to verbal or demonstrated guidance for transferring ideas into action
- Like to start projects and let others finish them

Socializers may succumb to their excitable tendencies. Concentrating on tasks and taking more logical approaches can help Socializers improve their follow through.

Relater Behavior in a Work Setting

Relaters prefer secure positions and careers in which they can specialize in some areas and be part of a team, such as the following:

- Financial adviser
- Social worker
- Health or community services worker
- Teacher
- Personal assistant/secretary
- Librarian
- Customer service representative

How Relaters Think

Relaters operate predominantly from a deductive perspective. Instead of naturally sensing (Director) or feeling (Socializer), Relaters think about things: "I think that something is really troubling John. His eyes are bloodshot, he's short-tempered and edgy, and he's been getting to work about an hour late for two days in a row." Even their feelings about others seem to be based on their thoughts about them. This ties in with Relaters' more concrete or literal orientations. They often need to see something with their own eyes before they are sure about it.

Relaters are extremely uncomfortable with conflict. In the workplace, people of this type notice how others complete their tasks; however, they typically say nothing negative (except possibly to a close friend or family member). Why? They don't want to make waves, and they don't want to appear to be know-it-alls. Silently, Relaters may think that they are shouldering the lion's share of duties, but they generally will not mention it to the boss or fellow employees. They will just continue performing their own work and make the best of it.

Both people factors and going along with established practices rate high with people of this type. When problems bombard Relaters, they try to solve them by helping or working with others, following tried-and-true procedures, or a combination of the two. If these tactics fail, Relaters may quietly do nothing. Doing nothing may include absenteeism; when conflict and stress increase, Relaters' tolerance may decrease.

As with any trait, Relaters' propensities for studying procedures and doing repetitious tasks can sometimes go to extremes. For instance, the following anecdote about the Relater type illustrates this point. After Michelangelo (a Thinker) completed the frescoes on the ceilings of the Sistine Chapel, the Pope asked him to draw up architectural plans for St. Peter's Cathedral. Because Michelangelo had passed his eightieth birthday, he drew up the massive and complex plans in less than two years. He then turned them over to his most promising apprentice, who happened to be a Relater. This slower-moving cohort's approach to implementing these plans was to study them step by step, day after day, year after year, time and again. Finally—after twenty-three years—he was ready to direct his efforts to the actual building of this world-famous cathedral.

How Relaters Work

When called on to make presentations, Relaters will probably thoroughly prepare and organize their material in advance. Because they feel comfortable with proven methods, Relaters like to acquaint themselves carefully with each step of a procedure so they can duplicate it later. When taken to extremes, this adherence to following instructions and maintaining the status quo can limit their actions.

Because Relaters are easygoing and favor step-by-step procedures, they are natural choices for assisting or tutoring others, maintaining existing performance levels, and organizing systems. They often enjoy helping to set up or to implement guidelines that help others to be more organized. Remember, Relaters are the ones who assemble all their equipment first, set up their tools, and begin to work only when everything is in place.

For instance, when she is preparing to collate reports, Relater Paula places all the pages in descending order on a table. Next, she places Tacky Finger on one side of the desk and a stapler with extra staples on the other side. She then clears a large space near page one for the completed stacks. When everything is ready, she begins to work on the completion of this task. Many a Director and Socializer who initially scoffed at what they viewed as laborious preparation later marveled at this assembly line efficiency. At this point, a sincere compliment on her work procedure might be both appropriate and welcome.

What Motivates Relaters

Because they are naturally interested listeners, Relaters appreciate these same behaviors from others. They like others who genuinely share a common interest in exchanging thoughts, feelings, and experiences. This sometimes takes some extra effort, however, because Relaters tend to speak indirectly. They seldom come right out and say what is on their minds, especially if they think something may be amiss.

In business and in their personal lives, Relaters take one day at a time and may consciously avoid gambles and uncertainties. They tend to respect traditions and often demonstrate loyalty to everyone else while they go along. Because stability in the workplace motivates them, Relaters are apt to have the most compatible of all working relationships with each of the four types. Relaters have patience, staying power, and persistence, so they commit themselves to making relationships work.

Relaters tend to gravitate toward relationships that provide them with security, stability, and large doses of routine; these positions satisfy some of their needs to nurture. Although not all teachers are Relaters, people of this type pursue careers that fit their natural desire for people contact, sameness, and opportunities to help or support others.

Because they are inherently modest and accommodating, Relaters usually think that their actions speak for themselves. When Directors and Socializers pat themselves on the backs, Relaters tend to simply nod and listen. Inwardly, they may want to divulge a personal triumph, but they will not volunteer it unless someone asks. Relaters tend to adopt a "Me last, if there's time" attitude. At work, Relaters may think they deserve promotions, but they are more likely to wait for the boss to notice than to bring it to the supervisor's attention.

Relater Leaders

Relater leaders go by the book—a manifestation of their deductive, convergent, left-brain orientations. They are driven by a basic need to use predictable, steady actions to yield known, proven results. At the most extreme, their battle cry is "Ready! Ready! Ready!" In fact, they might still be getting ready when the enemy fires. Then they may react by saying to others in their groups, "What's the SOP (standard operating procedure) for us to follow in this kind of situation?"

How to Approach Relaters

Because Relaters seek security and inclusion with a group, they can contribute to the workplace with their natural planning skills, consistent pace, and their desire to fit in. Like Socializers, they favor work relationships on a casual, first-name basis; but Relaters generally prefer developing special, more in-depth friendships with selected coworkers than do their Socializer counterparts. While Socializers may talk to anyone who will listen, Relaters prefer involvement with a closer group of confidants.

Relaters also want stability, steadiness, and a calm atmosphere in the workplace. They contribute to harmony in the office, so they usually fit comfortably into the work environment. However, they also often become too dependent on using the same old methods repeatedly.

⊕ **Remember** ⊕

Relaters' Business Characteristics

- Need to know the order of procedures
- Operate well as members of a work group
- Motivated by usual, known, and proven practices
- Oriented toward more concrete, repeatable actions
- Want order in the workplace
- Look for stability in the workplace
- Focus on how and when to do things
- Work in a steady and predictable manner
- Like long-term relationships with their companies
- Like long-term relationships with their coworkers

Relaters' Preferred Business Situations

- Like to perform the same kinds of duties each day
- Prefer to work cooperatively with others to achieve common results
- Dislike taking risks
- Enjoy working in a stable, steady, low-key environment
- Want a minimum of changes
- Like to know each step toward completing their duties
- Prefer to make decisions by group consensus
- Function according to standard operating procedures
- Prefer not to make decisions by themselves
- Enjoy feeling like valued members of the work group

Sometimes these procedures include steps needed when they first learned the procedure, but which can now be discarded. They may improve their work productivity by using shortcuts that eliminate extra labor. Directors and Socializers can often help them with this. And, when asked, Thinkers can generally demonstrate new ways to get things done through other processes.

Relaters are the optimistic realists among the four types. As pragmatists, they like to do routine things with familiar people to maintain the same situation. They perform regularly and deliberately to hold onto or strive for continuity, peace, and orderliness. Changes and surprises make Relaters uncomfortable because they alter the current formula. Instead, they prefer to refine existing practices.

Thinker Behavior in a Work Setting

Thinkers prefer careers in which they can strive for perfection, creativity, and completeness, such as the following:

- Forecasters (political, weather, etc.)
- Critics (film, history, literary, etc.)
- Research scientists
- Data analysts
- Accountants/auditors
- Artists/sculptors/architects
- Inventors

How Thinkers Think

Thinkers see themselves as problem solvers who like structure, concentrate on key details, and ask specific questions about identified factors. They are masters at following important, established directions and standards, while still meeting the need to control the process by their own actions. Process-oriented Thinkers want to know *why* something works; such insight allows them to determine for themselves the most logical ways to achieve the expected results—from themselves and others.

Thinkers rank second only to Relaters in their pursuit of logic. They rely on reasoning to avoid mistakes, and so they tend to check, recheck, and check again. But they may get mired down with data collection. While they are still amassing facts and specifics, Thinkers are uncomfortable giving opinions or partial information. This tendency can frustrate people with faster paces, who want to know what is going on now. In addition, all that extra checking can disrupt the work flow.

Thinkers can benefit from checking only critical elements instead of checking everything. This procedure allows them to sort out and control important details and still get things done well. They can hold onto their high standards without becoming bogged down in trivial business details. Thinkers need to learn to accept that perfection is an impossible quest—worth the effort in some cases, but not in others.

How Thinkers Work

In business, Thinkers are practical and realistic. They seek neither utopias nor quick fixes. Because Thinkers have low risk-taking tendencies, they may plan too much when change becomes inevitable. They like working in existing circumstances that promote quality in products or services. When possible, they prepare ahead of time for their projects and then work diligently to perfect them. Thorough preparation is designed to minimize the probability of errors. They prefer finishing tasks before or on schedule without mistakes caused by last-minute rushing and inadequate checking or review.

When airline pilots prepare to fly a commercial plane, they have a checklist of safety points before takeoff. Thinker pilots have been found to focus far more on the most critical factors, using the remaining time to review the less crucial ones. In typical Thinker style, they complete the checklist by checking known factors against unknown variables. By contrast, Director pilots might delegate this duty to others. In this way, they see to it that the task gets done. Socializer pilots have been observed getting off task by talking to coworkers who come in during this process. Then they may wait until the last minute to finish because of the difficulty they have in assessing the amount of time needed to complete such detailed tasks. Relaters go through each point, in the listed order, completing it in a step-by-step way, but without the same rigorous attention that Thinkers apply to the most critical items. Although all four types finish the checklist, they complete this task quite differently—according to their different styles—and with the possibility of different outcomes.

What Motivates Thinkers

Whether or not people of this type opt for scientific or artistic careers, they often follow scientific methods or intuitive, logical progressions to achieve their objectives. Because of their natural inclination to validate and improve upon accepted processes, Thinkers tend to generate the most native creativity of the four types. Consequently, they often find new ways of viewing old questions, concerns, and opportunities.

Many artists and inventors fall into the Thinker category; many lean toward experimentation and the possibility of coming up with new answers. Just as Michelangelo's creative mind envisioned completed sculptures entrapped in solid pieces of marble, Leonardo da Vinci's technique for perfecting Mona Lisa's expression still baffles experts. Similarly, Galileo's creativity formulated precisely detailed plans of "impossible" futuristic inventions. These three Renaissance men left lasting memorials as evidence of the quality-consciousness often associated with Thinker tendencies.

Thinker Leaders

Thinker leaders tend to be private people who exhibit calm, cool, objective behaviors that detractors view as aloofness and insensitivity. They use planned, careful actions to achieve their desired results.

Because Thinkers often detect complexities that escape other people, they can become perfectionistic and worrisome, with both themselves and others. Although this quality-control aspect can be very positive, associates may dismiss the caution as immaterial if it is taken to

extremes. When Thinkers are willing to bend their standards on small matters, coworkers are more likely to listen
to them for the bigger issues.

How to Approach Thinkers

Like Relaters, Thinkers are basically introverted individuals who seek solace and answers by turning inward.
Thinkers' natural orientation is toward objects and away
from people. From the Thinker's perspective, people are
unpredictable, and they complicate things. The more
people who are added to the mix, the greater the chance
of getting unpredictable results.

Thinkers often choose to work with colleagues who
promote calmness and thoroughness in the office—often
either other Thinkers or Relaters. Because Thinkers seek
perfection, the other types may help them modify that
quest into a more time-efficient procedure. Directors can
contribute by helping to explain realistic deadlines and
parameters, so Thinkers can build those time frames into
their procedures. Socializers, too, can help them lighten
up more at work and teach them that there is more to the
workplace than working alone eight hours a day.

When encouraged to do so, Thinkers can share their
rich supplies of information with small groups of coworkers who can benefit from their wealth of experience and
knowledge. This can enhance Thinkers' status with colleagues and become a bridge toward building teamwork
and mutual understanding. Sharing with others can also
serve to lessen Thinkers' reservations and suspicions
about associates or even encourage them to stand up
for themselves against the very people they may prefer
to avoid.

✤ **Remember** ✤

Thinkers' Business Characteristics

- Concerned with processes
- Want to know *how* things work
- Think intuitively and originally
- May invent their own structures, methods, or models
- Value quality over quantity
- Prefer lower output to inferior results
- Employ logical thinking process to avoid mistakes
- Over-attend to details, sometimes impeding progress
- Dislike changes and surprises
- Reject aggression

Thinkers' Preferred Business Situations

- Want appreciation of their work or ideas from supervisors
- Avoid criticism of their work
- Like to set the quality-control standards
- Monitor standards to be sure that they are implemented properly
- Work with complete data systems
- Able to formulate some data systems themselves
- Want to be valued by supervisors for correctness
- Prefer workplaces that are organized and process oriented
- Minimize socializing in the workplace
- Want to be seen as key workers in the organization

Because Thinkers want clarity and order, they can contribute a natural sense of thoroughness. They usually do not care about knowing the name of each person in the department; however, they may choose to find out more about people who exhibit the same thoroughness and precision they themselves exhibit.

Thinkers want peace and tranquillity; they avoid and reject hostility and outward expressions of aggression. At the extreme, they can numb themselves to conflict so much that they have difficulty tapping into feelings— caring and love as well as anger and hatred.

By learning to accept others' expressions of emotions, Thinkers can also learn to accept their own feelings. Ideally, if Thinkers can consciously raise their tolerance for aggression, they can then begin to increase their abilities to deal with it successfully.

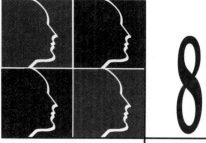

8

Leadership Styles

Making This Chapter Meaningful to You

Picture a Director, Socializer, Relater, and Thinker with whom you work. As you read this chapter, bear in mind each of these particular people and garner what you can do to improve your relationships. For each person, focus both on his or her more productive traits and the less productive ones.

A common universal leadership language exists around the world in management circles. Whether you are a corporate president, head of a small company, a board member, director of a nonprofit organization, an independent consultant, or senior pastor of a church, you can greatly increase your effectiveness as a leader by learning to speak this language. It involves the most widely known leadership concept in continued practice today, the managerial grid, which reveals a person's leadership-influencing approach.

The essence of this idea is that all people have their own natural, preferred ways to do things; this includes how they exert influence over people and/or manage tasks or organizations. In their styles of leadership, Directors are the most observably directive of the types. On the other hand, Socializers are the most naturally supportive in the way they go about their efforts to influence others and manage situations. By contrast, Relaters and Thinkers are more introverted by nature and less easily identifiable in their leadership practices. Relaters, in their quest to be liked, are similar to the supportive Socializers; the difference would be that for Relaters, being supportive is secondary to providing the expected service or accomplishing a certain result. Finally, Thinkers are similar to self-determined Directors; the difference is that Thinkers would rather achieve their standards without annoying others.

Toward Appropriate Management

When Don Cipriano, top salesperson worldwide for Performax International, conducted a session on Motivational Management in London, he said, "We manage people the way they need to be managed, not the way we want to manage." One manager commented that idea really hit home because his high Director behavior was creating some problems with the Relaters and Thinkers on the staff. This manager began to run his office according to the way his staff needed to be managed, with great success; however, he did not have the same success with a certain new employee. One day, that employee made an appointment with the manager and told him, "If you'd stop wasting time providing all those details, I could get my work done."

This manager had made the mistake of being so accustomed to managing Relaters and Thinkers that he failed to recognize the new employee's Director behaviors. The manager later said to Cipriano, "I fell into the same trap again, managing everyone the same way."

Similarly, when Dr. John Lee, a renowned time management expert, conducts workshops, he often asks, "What is the operating philosophy of your company?" He says that presidents of organizations seem surprised when they hear the diversity of answers mentioned by their staff members. If the leader does not verbalize, clarify, and gather input about what direction everyone is working toward, how can the company function smoothly?

Director Leaders: Move Over and Let Them Do Their Thing

Directors are like wild horses that do not run in rigid formation. Why hobble them if they can get blue ribbons in their own way? Or if they can start and develop their own herd? If you confine them, Directors may become harsh and stubborn; let them do their own thing and they may very well impress you. Agree on the goals and specify the boundaries of the playing field—then get out of their way.

This approach requires that other people look beyond the natural competitive spirit of Directors and instead focus this energy on a common goal for bettering the organization. Directors seek this sort of encouragement and feedback to function most effectively within the general framework of shared expectations. But don't expect them to follow every procedure to the letter.

Coaching Directors

When coaching Directors, remember that they like to learn basic steps and quickly sift out what they want to know. In the interest of saving time, Directors may try to find shortcuts; show them the simplest, fastest route to the desired destination. Give them the bottom line and then let them go. To help them to be more efficient, give them parameters, guidelines, and deadlines.

For Directors, the thought of reassuring someone or explaining something more than once is frittering away precious moments that they would rather spend on action and results. They would rather not bother with details. Focus attention on the high points, such as what they need to do and when it is due. Directors want only to know those details required to get something to function so that they can then turn to other important new opportunities—like making money, for instance. Instead of covering steps one through twenty-four, Directors prefer to hear only about the key steps. Forcing Directors to sit through all twenty-four points would be like torture to them. This lack of attention to details can result in their searching for new ways to streamline routine jobs to get the desired effects more readily.

Managing Directors is no easy task because they want to manage you! You can squelch them, or you can encourage them to take control of certain arenas. Work with Directors' strengths by allowing them to take charge, where qualified, on particular projects. Their preferences for change and innovation make them natural choices for new programs in which they can implement their own ideas. Make sure that the Directors understand that they need to check with you at specific intervals, or they may show the "renegade syndrome"—doing things their own way, without answering to anyone else.

Communicating With Directors

Be prepared to listen to Directors' suggestions, the course of action they have in mind, and/or the general results they are considering. This enables you to begin on a positive note by indicating the areas in which you already agree. Then you can work backward toward gaining agreement on the results that you both want—and that you are willing to either mutually or independently allow the other to achieve.

Describe to Directors the results that you want, showing them the gap between actual and desired results. Suggest clearly the needed improvement and establish a time when they will get back to you.

When offering them different ideas, opinions, or actions, be sure to point out that you are trying to work in ways that are acceptable to them—and also to yourself. Focus on your intent to identify solutions that will also meet their expectations. Stress that you do not want to cause difficulties for yourself or for them.

Directors will want to present their own initial views of the decision to be made or problem to be solved and the process they prefer to follow in reaching a clear-cut (and preferably quickly chosen) solution.

Directors tend to make autonomous, no-nonsense decisions. If the decision will help them to meet their goals, they will agree; if not, they typically will say "no." People of this type will procrastinate in reaching a conclusion when it will take too much time or effort to do the homework to find the best alternative. You can prevent this procrastination by simply providing a brief analysis for each option you present to Directors. Provide them with options and clearly describe the probabilities of success in achieving goals.

Counseling Directors

When counseling Directors, stick to the facts. Draw out Directors by talking about the desired results, and then

✛ **Action Plan** ✛

When You Are the Director

- Allow others to do things without excessive or untimely interference
- Participate in the group without expecting always to be in command
- Modify your tendency to give orders to others
- Enlist others' input and support through participative, collaborative actions
- Give others credit when they deserve it
- Praise people for jobs well done
- Let colleagues and employees know that you realize that mistakes are to be expected
- Give authority as well as responsibility when delegating

When Others Are Directors, Help Them Learn to:

- Gauge risks more realistically
- Exercise more caution and deliberation before making decisions and coming to conclusions
- Follow pertinent rules, regulations, and expectations
- Recognize and solicit others' contributions, both as individuals and within a group
- Tell others the reasons for decisions
- Cultivate more attention/responsiveness to emotions

discuss their concerns. Focus on tasks more than feelings, and ask them how they would solve the problem.

Motivating Directors

Compared to the other types, Directors are more likely to thrive in pressure-cooker situations. They naturally gravitate toward those power positions and career areas in which they can take charge—as executives, politicians, military officers, stockbrokers, or newspaper reporters. Winning, more than anything else, motivates this type.

When it is appropriate to reward or reinforce their behaviors, focus on how pleased you are. Point out their achievements, upward mobility, and leadership potential. Assume that Directors are also pleased with achieving the desired outcomes, so omit personal comments and focus on their track record. Mention how glad you are to be working with them to make things better for both of you through cooperation. The bottom line? Each of you gets better results by combining your energies on a common targeted goal.

Socializer Leaders: Help Them Focus Their Abilities

With their boundless energy and enthusiasm, Socializers can get involved with so many different activities that they may accomplish goals with a flourish. Or, they may show flurries of activity without accomplishing things in the most efficient way. Managers and coworkers can help channel that energy and enthusiasm with tactful reminders and hands-on assistance to help them to set priorities and to organize. Then, the entire office may function more smoothly. Because Socializers tend to be open, people of other types often can detect when Socializers are having off days and give them verbal boosts with compliments and personal attention.

Coaching Socializers

When coaching Socializers, avoid giving them too much at once or they will become overwhelmed. Skip as much of the detailed, tedious information as possible. Get them involved. Socializers are typically kinesthetic, hands-on learners. Let them first get a feel for what is needed, then show you what they understand so that you can give them structured feedback. Frequently, people of this type want to jump in and try before they are ready or before they fully understand everything. Allow them to save face when they do something wrong, and be generous with compliments when they get it right.

Many Socializers find that sorting out priorities and solutions becomes very difficult when too many opportunities bombard them. When this happens, they may become uncharacteristically mute and immobilized— temporarily, of course. Other people can help by setting priorities for Socializers to tackle. This approach enables Socializers to separate their feelings from the facts and from other people's expectations. Ironically, when Socializers' tasks become more organized, their anxiety levels lessen—despite the fact that they bristle at the thought of organizing. Socializers cannot be all things to all people; focusing and refocusing on what is really important is essential to a sense of well-being.

Socializers are often idea people who have plenty of ideas, but not necessarily the means of carrying them out. Steer them toward ways of assuring that those ideas are implemented. Praise the work done thus far, tell them where to go for more facts, encourage participative exchanges with coworkers, explain the parameters, and show them how to stay on track. Structure tasks to fit the natural work style of each person. As one bumper sticker advises, "Never teach a duck to sing. It's a waste of time, and it annoys the duck."

Communicating With Socializers

Get ready to act enthusiastically with Socializers. Show them that you are interested in them by letting them talk and by using more animation in your own gestures and voice. Illustrate your ideas with stories or mental pictures that relate to them and their goals. Socializers like to interact with people, so try not to hurry your discussion. Include opportunities for small talk and getting personally acquainted.

Socializers operate predominantly from a multiple-focus, right-brain perspective. They see mental pictures first, then convert those pictures to words. Preferring main ideas and generalities to details, Socializers base decisions on their impulses, feelings, and others' recommendations and testimonials. For people of this behavioral type, emotions rule. This does not mean that they never use logic or facts; rather, feelings and emotions come first. For Socializers, thinking processes are the servants to their feelings.

Socializers like to envision the big picture. Because they generally are less motivated by facts and details, they respond better to short overviews or capsule summaries of what you plan to cover. Attempt to develop some stimulating, enjoyable ideas together while focusing on their opinions and dreams. Socializers turn off to people who douse their dreams. Support their ideas while showing them how they can transfer their talk into actions.

If you disagree, try not to argue because Socializers dislike conflict. You are not likely to win arguments with them anyway because their strong suit is feelings and intuition. If trapped, Socializers can twist people around and manipulate feelings with their use of words and emotions. Instead of arguing, try to explore alternate solutions. When you reach agreement, spell out the specific details concerning what, when, who, and how. Then document the agreement with them so that they will not forget the details.

When delegating work to Socializers, make sure to receive clear agreement. Set up checkpoints/times to avoid long stretches with no progress reports. Otherwise, they may lapse into their natural way of doing things—spontaneously completing particular items that feel best while postponing less stimulating tasks, especially those that involve follow-up and checking.

Counseling Socializers

Give Socializers enough time to talk about whatever may be bothering them. Pay attention to both facts and feelings, but put your primary emphasis on their feelings. Ask probing questions and involve them by asking how they could solve the challenge or difficulty. Sometimes just airing their feelings and thoughts relieves tension for these individuals. Talking allows them to vent their frustrations and can even become an end in itself, inasmuch as the quality of their relationships influences their energy levels.

When stress hits Socializers, they prefer to look the other way and search for more positive, upbeat experiences. They avoid problems for as long as they can. If the pressure persists, they tend literally to walk away from the problem. When these tactics fail, they may panic.

Be prepared to listen to their personal feelings and experiences, because they need to be both expressive and able to share their emotions with others. Their style requires open and responsive interaction with others, preferably by way of congenial and unhurried conversation.

Socializers will want to avoid a discussion of more complex, negative-sounding or otherwise messy problem situations. It is difficult for them to feel positive with you or anyone else under such circumstances. Let them know specifically what the problem behaviors happen to be. Define the behaviors that can eliminate problems and confirm mutually agreeable action plans in writing to prevent future misunderstandings. Because Socializers prefer to keep conversations light, avoid what they view as negative or distasteful approaches. Use optimistically stated questions, because Socializers would simply rather deal with things that are going right.

In making decisions with them, they will be open to your suggestions—as long as these ideas will allow them to look and feel good—and not require much difficult, follow-up, detail work or long-term commitments. When suggesting different ideas, opinions, or actions to them, be sure to point out you are doing it that way if it will be acceptable to them. Focus on your desire to identify solutions that also will meet their expectations. Stress that you do not want to cause difficulties for yourself or for them.

Above all, offer your suggestions as gifts that can make this situation (task or relationship) easier and more beneficial to them—as well as to others.

Motivating Socializers

Socializers like special packages and extras to inspire them to full effort. Show them how they can look good in the eyes of others. Many businesses use yearly contests to motivate their employees. In these situations, Socializers tend to sprint toward a quick win—for the first week or two. Then they may get sidetracked by other things and do nothing more about it until a week before the contest ends. If they can get excited enough, they may win the contest anyway; however, the truth is they have not worked toward that goal for most of the year. How can these types keep up their motivation? Because Socializers like constant rewards along the way, they may favor shorter contests with smaller payoffs, perhaps culminating in the big one when the year ends. Or, Socializers may enlist assistance from other colleagues who are better at implementation than they are.

Pay direct personal compliments to Socializers as individuals when they legitimately deserve them. Mention their charm, friendliness, creative ideas, persuasiveness, and/or appearance (or better yet, all of the above). Unlike people of other types, who respond to more specific job-related comments, Socializers mentally relive more global generalizations for weeks to come.

When it is appropriate to reward or reinforce their behaviors, focus on how glad you are that they have succeeded in finding solutions to their concerns or objectives. In addition, let Socializers know how much you appreciate them for their openness and willingness to be responsive.

⊹ **Action Plan** ⊹

When You Are the Socializer

- Attend to key details, when appropriate
- Improve your follow-through efforts
- Monitor socializing to keep it in balance with other aspects of life
- Write things down and work from a list, so you will know what to do when
- Set priorities for activities and focus on tasks in their order of importance
- Become more organized and orderly in the way you do things
- Get the less appealing tasks of the day finished early
- Pay more attention to time management of activities
- Check to make sure you are on course with known tasks or goals

When Others Are Socializers, Help Them Learn to:

- Set priorities and organize
- See tasks through to completion
- View people and tasks more objectively
- Avoid the overuse of giving and taking advice, which can result in lack of focus on task
- Write things down
- Do the unpleasant as well as the fun things
- Focus on what is important now
- Avoid procrastination and/or hoping others will do things for them

By now, you realize that Socializers exhibit natural talkativeness and ease with people. This makes them good choices for maintaining group morale and motivation. They think aloud and enjoy participating in brainstorming sessions anyway, so why not get their opinions and assistance on recognition awards, entertainment, or fund-raising activities? They strive for recognition, so activities that attract attention appeal to them.

Relater Leaders: Encourage Them to Update Their Methods

Relaters contribute stability and perseverance to their workplaces. Because they work toward harmony in the office, they usually fit comfortably into the work environment; however, they may become used to using the same old methods repeatedly. Sometimes their procedures include steps that were needed when they learned the procedure, but which now can be discarded. They may improve their work practices by using shortcuts that eliminate extra steps. Directors and Socializers can often help them with this. And, when asked, Thinkers also can generally suggest new ways to get things done.

Coaching Relaters

When Relaters are in training for jobs, they favor one-on-one, hands-on instruction with a real person, starting at the beginning and ending at the end. When they learn each step, Relaters generally are more comfortable with their functions. During training and in other newer situations, Relaters tend to observe others for a longer-than-average time. When they feel they can do the task, then and only then will they comfortably begin. This slower pace can frustrate Directors and Socializers, both of whom like to plunge right in. Understanding that Relaters need to do things slowly can reassure the faster-paced types that the job will get done.

Get ready to be ready with Relaters. Have a step-by-step list of procedures or a working timetable/schedule at your disposal. Relaters need to feel secure in their mastery of procedures until their actions become second nature and more routine. At the same time, they prefer a pleasant and patient approach while they learn what you expect of them.

Communicating With Relaters

Be ready to do more talking than listening with Relaters, because they do not naturally feel comfortable when the limelight focuses on them. You will want to clarify any key agenda items with them, working to stay organized and moving forward steadily but slowly as you check to make sure they both understand and accept what you say.

In dealing with problems and decisions with Relaters, make sure to deal with only one subject or situation at a time, one step at a time. To gain clarity, before moving on to other items, make sure they are ready, willing, and able to do so. Recalling that they need stability, deal with matters in a calm and relaxed manner. Encourage them to share their suggestions about how to make the decision in a way that is likely to add even more stability to the current conditions.

When suggesting different possibilities to Relaters, point out how you are trying to identify ways that you can help continue to make things pleasant for them. You simply have ideas or opinions that will help stabilize your own relationship expectations with them and that are important to you, too.

Relaters may be reluctant to ask others to do their own share of the work. You could make a personal appeal to their loyalty and sense of fair play. Give them the task, state the deadlines, and explain why it is important to do it that way.

Counseling Relaters

Allow plenty of time for Relaters to explore their thoughts and feelings so you can understand the emotional sides of the situation. Relaters usually express their feelings less directly, so draw them out through questioning and listening to their responses. Bear in mind that people of this type tend to balk at sudden change, whether the change is good or bad. The key point is that the unknown disrupts their stability-motivated state. You can help reduce their fears by showing how specific changes will benefit them and the company.

Reassure them that you only want to correct specific behaviors. Relaters tend to take things personally, so remove the "something is wrong with you" barrier as quickly as possible. Avoid blaming or judging Relaters; keep the conversation focused on behaviors and their appropriateness. If the problem involves procedures, help them learn how to improve. Point out in nonthreatening ways what they are already doing right while also emphasizing what needs to change.

Motivating Relaters

Besides thinking that they can learn to master a series of procedures, Relaters like to feel that their relationships

⊕ **Action Plan** ⊕

When You Are the Relater

- Stretch by taking on a bit more (or different) duties beyond your comfort level
- Increase how often you verbalize your thoughts and feelings
- Speed up your actions by getting into some projects more quickly
- Desensitize yourselves somewhat, so that your colleagues' feelings do not affect your own performance
- Learn to adapt more quickly to either changes or refinements of existing practices
- Bolster your assertiveness techniques

**When Others Are Relaters,
Help Them Learn to:**

- Use shortcuts and discard unnecessary steps
- Track their growth
- Avoid doing things the same way
- Focus on goals without attending to other thoughts or feelings
- Realize that there is more than one approach to tasks
- Become more open to risk and change
- Feel sincerely appreciated
- Speak up and voice their thoughts and feelings
- Modify their tendencies to do what others tell them to do
- Get and accept credit and praise, when appropriate

with others can benefit from their follow-through. Mention their teamwork and dependability. Remark about how others regard them, how well they get along with coworkers, and how important their efforts to build relationships have been to the company. Effusiveness can arouse the suspicions of Relaters, so stick to praising what they have done rather than praising their more abstract, personal attributes. Otherwise, their modesty and your vagueness may cause them to dismiss your comments.

To reward or reinforce Relaters' behaviors, focus on appreciating their willingness to work to make things good for you and others. Approach matters in a systematic, low-key, and understandable manner. Point out that they make important contributions when they take the initiative to share their own ideas, interests, and insights in helping to ensure results.

Thinker Leaders: Help Them Substitute Quality for Perfection

Coaching Thinkers

When coaching Thinkers, point out the most important things to remember first. Then demonstrate procedures efficiently and logically, stressing the purpose of each step. Go at a relatively slow pace, stopping at each key place in the process to check for their understanding. Ask for possible input, especially regarding refinements that may be appropriate. This approach ensures success with the task and minimizes Thinkers' stress levels.

Communicating With Thinkers

Because Thinkers have complex thinking patterns, they base decisions on proven information and track records. They want to make rational choices based on facts, not on other people's opinions or testimonials—unless those people are those Thinkers' personal heroes.

Even with testimonials they value, they'll probably want to see facts in writing. When Thinkers say, "I need to think about it," they usually mean it. You can help them to make a decision by supplying the materials they request and by allowing them the time to make the right decisions for themselves. Focus on emphasizing deadlines and parameters so that Thinkers can build those time frames into their procedures.

Be well organized and clear in your communications, because Thinkers are likely to ask many questions about a situation or subject in their search for logical conclusions. You may want to have them clarify their more pressing concerns. Ask your questions in a discreet, nonjudgmental manner to elicit the points, objectives, or assurances Thinkers want.

Set the stage for communication by making sure that they are open to discussing the problem or decision being considered at this time. If they are not ready, either set a definite time that is better for both of you or explore their concerns about pursuing this subject. When you explore the situation itself, review your impression of the entire process. Choose a logical approach for agreeing about both the problem or decision involved and the most reasonable way of resolving it. Do so in a way that is likely to be most satisfactory to them, you, and any other key individuals involved.

When suggesting different possibilities to Thinkers, point out how you want to identify ideas, perspectives, or actions that allow you, them, and others to reach better solutions or situations. Stress how fewer difficulties or less confusion can result. Ask them what insights and suggestions they, or individuals they know and value, could bring to this situation.

Take time to answer their most critical questions about structure and/or guidance they require in specific situations. The more Thinkers understand the details, the more likely they will be to complete the task properly. Be sure to establish deadlines.

Counseling Thinkers

Elicit their thoughts about processes, procedures or problems. Like Relaters, Thinkers often express their thoughts and opinions indirectly, so persist in your attempts to get them to talk. People of this type dislike change because they typically view changes and the future as unknown variables where unforeseen mistakes might happen. They need to plan for change ahead of time so they can identify and bring under control any key considerations that have to be addressed in the process. When possible, allow them to investigate possible repercussions, especially at the beginning stages. That way they will know more about the future and may be more comfortable with possible changes.

Show Thinkers the way to get a job done and they typically will master the format, then modify it to suit their individual needs. They tend to start with what they have to work with, then personalize it, almost from the beginning, so that it works better as they see it. They may avoid people whom they perceive might tell them to do things differently. This is one way that Thinkers maintain control of their work. They tend to sidestep authorities who attempt to correct them. At the extreme, this behavior can appear sneaky to others.

To correct Thinkers, specify exact behaviors and outline how you would like to see them changed. Establish agreed-on checkpoints and times. Allow them to save face, as they fear being wrong.

Motivating Thinkers

Appeal to Thinkers' needs for accuracy and logic. People of this type do not respond well to fancy verbal antics, so keep your approach clear. Better yet, provide illustration and documentation. Avoid exaggeration and vagueness. Show them how this is the best available current option.

If Thinkers decide to take part in a competitive situation, they'll probably do it as they do other tasks—bit by bit—until they do it right. Unlike their colleagues who may show enthusiasm at the beginning, Thinkers often show the patience and follow-through to ultimately win—if they perceive the contest as worthwhile and do not become too preoccupied with details along the way. Whereas some people focus on winning shorter-term battles, Thinkers are motivated by the ultimate sense of lasting personal glory derived from triumphing in the total war.

Mention their efficiency, thought processes, organization, persistence, and accuracy. Do not mix personal and professional comments except with Thinkers you know very well. Even then, they prefer more privately communicated, plausible praise. Keep praise simple and concise for Thinkers.

✣ **Action Plan** ✣

When You Are the Thinker

- Modify your criticism (whether spoken or unspoken) of others' work
- Check less often, or only check the critical things (as opposed to everything), allowing the flow of the process to continue
- Ease up on Self-Contained emotions; engage in more casual interactions
- Accept the fact that you can have high standards without expecting perfection
- Occasionally confront a colleague (or boss) with whom you disagree, instead of avoiding or ignoring them (and doing what you want to do anyway)
- Tone down the tendency to over-prepare

When Others Are Thinkers,
Help Them Learn to:

- Share their knowledge and expertise with others
- Stand up for themselves with the people they prefer to avoid
- Shoot for realistic deadlines and parameters
- View people and tasks less seriously and critically
- Balance their lives with both interaction and tasks
- Keep on course with tasks, with less checking
- Maintain high expectations for high-priority items, but not necessarily for everything

Focus on your realization of how difficult it can be at times for Thinkers to attempt to meet the high personal standards they set for themselves. Also focus on how much you appreciate this personal characteristic for what it has done to make things better for you in your relationships with them. Cite specific and appropriate examples that prove this point. Then, notice their reactions. If they appear uncomfortable, share with them that you did not mean to cause embarrassment, but just to let them know how much you value them. If the reaction you get is more positive, ask them to tell you more about the sense of satisfaction and enjoyment they derive from similar things.

The "Best" Leadership Style

Remember, there is no such thing as the best, all-purpose leadership style. Instead, the best leaders are those who realize what a job, role, or specific situation requires for successful performance and then ensure those outcomes. At times, this may involve a clear-cut match between your own strengths and the required actions. At other times, behavior requirements may vary. Effective leaders adapt their own natural styles by using new behavior methods or calling on other qualified individuals whose talents and energies can contribute to handling the immediate problem. Good leaders also may take action to modify the environment. This could include shifting the work priorities to ensure the successful completion of the necessary task without sacrificing the well-being of other people. Productivity will be maximized by using these breakthrough leadership techniques and options.

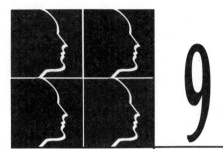

9

Selling and Servicing With Style!

Using Styles in Sales and Service

Every sales or service call has certain similarities; however, technique differentiates professional salespeople from other salespeople. Professionals focus more on helping than selling, more on listening than talking, more on problem solving than persuading, more on creating long-term customers than one-time sales. The techniques used by professionals are simple yet powerful. Salespeople who use these techniques concentrate on a collaborative process that allows both the customer and the salesperson to feel good about the sales/service exchange and about each other. Professional sales and service staff always go through five specific steps, although the overall approach may vary depending on the behavioral styles of their prospects. You can apply the tips in this chapter to help you maximize your sales and service encounters, whether you fill the role of buyer or seller.

Think of someone you know in a sales or service situation who sounds like a Director, Socializer, Relater, and Thinker. How can you benefit with each one of them in a business relationship?

Five Steps to Selling and Servicing With Style

Step #1: Making Contact

The purpose of talking with your prospect is to begin building a business relationship by opening up lines of communication. Professional salespeople know that a solid business relationship goes beyond the immediate

175

product or service being offered. The relationship, and therefore the sale, requires establishing trust and building competence, confidence, and credibility. When prospects know that you sincerely have their best interests at heart, the rest of the process can continue. Today's buyers are appreciative of professionals who show an interest in them, their businesses, and their lives.

Step #2: Exploring Needs

Professional sales and service people spend a great deal of time exploring their prospects' needs. They look not only for needs but also for opportunities. Searching just for needs implies that customers only have problems that must be solved. Looking for or creating opportunities puts the salesperson in the position of a consultant who can take someone's current conditions and improve on them. Successful professionals encourage the prospect to become involved in this exploratory process. By asking well-structured questions and studying the many facets of the prospect's situation, you can build cooperation and a foundation for shared commitment.

Step #3: Proposing Solutions

After meeting with the potential customer and exploring his or her situation, the next step is to collaborate on options and propose solutions to the problem. The professional approach is one in which both parties work together toward a solution that is custom tailored to that prospect's needs. Because of the comprehensive collaboration you have had with the prospect, the benefits of the proposed solution naturally emerge as they relate to specific problems.

Step #4: Gaining Commitment

This is a logical conclusion to the ongoing communication and agreement that has been taking place with the prospect. Because the salesperson and the prospect have worked together on a common goal since the beginning, it is less likely that objections would be voiced at this point. Details may need to be worked out, but they usually will not get in the way. For professional sales and service people, the confirmation becomes a question of *when*, not *if*. If resistance occurs, it simply indicates a need to gather more information or clarify details. Gaps in communication are not a problem because experienced salespeople are willing to spend time with the prospect until everything is understood and accepted.

Step #5: Assuring Satisfaction

Professional sales and service people thrive on satisfied customers and see them for what they are—long-term assets! These veterans begin assuring customer satisfaction after the sale by changing roles from salespeople to quality service providers. They make sure the customer receives the proper order on the right delivery date. They also help the customer track the results and analyze the effectiveness of the product or service for the specific problem(s) addressed. By assuring the satisfaction of each customer, professionals build a clientele that guarantees future business and referrals.

How to Sell Your Product or Service to Directors

Directors want to know the bottom line. "What will this do for me?" and "By when?" Give them just enough information to satisfy their need to know about overall performance. They do not want to waste time reconstructing the product bolt by bolt, hearing a list of testimonials about your other satisfied clients, or getting to be fast friends. Even if you do not consider yourself a salesperson per se, remember that everyone sells something every day—whether ideas, integrity, credentials, image, or a less-than-palatable-looking picnic lunch. Regardless of your work, you can probably apply to your everyday life a few sales tips that typically work with Directors.

Step #1: Making Contact With the Director

When you write, call, or meet a Director, do it in a formal, businesslike manner. Get right to the point. Focus quickly on the task. Refer to bottom-line results, increased efficiency, saved time, return on investment, profits, and so on.

Take care to be well-organized, time conscious, efficient, and businesslike. Directors will be impatient with a slow pace, but they will become especially wary if they question a person's competence.

As a sales or service person, it is your job to provide both sufficient information and enough incentive for a Director to meet with you. When you call, you might say, "Some of the ways I thought we would be able to work together are X, Y, and Z. Could we discuss those when I call you at a time of your choice?" By planting a seed, you may raise the Director's interest level and the priority of your next call, unless, of course, the person just is not interested. Because individuals who fit this type pride themselves in being busy, they dislike granting several meetings. But if they think that time spent now will save time later, they are likely to explore matters with you now rather than later.

Step #2: Studying Directors' Needs

To head off Directors' impatience before it surfaces, alternately ask questions and give additional information. Do this in a practical manner. Directors need to view the meeting as purposeful, so they want to understand where your questions ultimately lead. When preparing questions for Directors, it is essential to fine-tune and make them as practical and logical as possible. Aim questions at the heart of the issue and ask them in a straightforward manner. Take care only to request information that is unavailable elsewhere.

When gathering information, ask questions that show that you have done your homework about the results they seek and their current efforts. Know the industry and company. Be sure to make queries that allow them to talk about their business goals. "Inasmuch as your leadership has brought your company from 27th to 3rd in the country, what happens now?" Gear your studying toward saving Directors time.

Step #3: Proposing Solutions for Directors

Your presentation must be geared toward the Directors' priorities. They are concerned with saving time, generating money, and making life easier and more efficient. Zero in on the bottom line with quick benefit statements. Because of their lack of time, Directors do not focus as much energy on contemplating and evaluating ideas. They want you to do the analysis and lay it out for them to approve or disapprove. Directors like rapid, concise analyses of their needs and your solutions. In addition, demonstrate your competence and show them how your product or service will help them achieve their goals. Focus on results and highlight important specifics. Cut out intermediate steps when you make your presentation, eliminate the small talk, and stick to business. Professionalism counts with Directors. During those times when it is appropriate to give historical data about your company or a more detailed presentation, write it out before you call. Highlight key points with a marking pen in advance, rather than burying them in a mass of paperwork. Skip over less important facts and show them the bottom-line basics. Then leave a copy of the information with them so they can refresh their memories later. Or Directors may want to delegate the fact checking to someone who really enjoys it—a Thinker or Relater.

Step #4: Gaining Commitment With Directors

With Directors, you can come right out and ask whether or not they are interested. You might say, "Based on what we've just discussed, are you interested in starting our service or carrying our product?" Directors will often answer you in no uncertain terms. At times, though, people of this type might put you off as if they cannot make a decision, when, in fact, they are not even thinking about your proposal. Directors can become so preoccupied with other business that they literally do not have the time to evaluate your ideas, especially if they do not have enough information.

The best way to deal with Directors is to give them options and probable outcomes. Bear in mind that Directors like to balance quality with cost considerations, so include this information when you want them to make decisions. Then offer options with supporting evidence and leave the final decisions to them. "The way I see it, you can go with Option A (tell pros and cons), Option B (more pros and cons), or Option C (still more pros and cons). I've outlined these three plans, costs of implementation, and approximate completion dates. Which one sounds best to you?" Directors seek control, so let them make the final decisions.

Step #5: Assuring Directors' Satisfaction

Because Directors usually do not emphasize personal relationships in business, you cannot rely on past sales to ensure future purchases. Follow up with Directors to find if they have any complaints or problems with your product. If they do, address these concerns immediately or their impatience may motivate them to seek help elsewhere, probably with another company.

Impress on your prospects that you intend to stand behind your product or service. Further, stress that you will follow up without taking a lot of their time. "You're buying this to save effort and time. I want to make sure it continues to work for you. I'll periodically check back to make sure everything is running smoothly, but I don't want to waste your time with unnecessary calls. When I telephone, if everything is fine, just say so and that will be it. If anything is less than what you expect, I want you to call me right away and I'll see to it the problem is fixed immediately." You may also want to offer a money-back guarantee: "If you aren't satisfied that you got your money's worth, I will personally take back the merchandise and write you a check."

Sales and Service Strategies for Dealing With Directors

- Plan to be prepared, organized, fast-paced, and to the point.
- Meet them in a professional and businesslike manner.
- Learn and study their goals and objectives—what they want to accomplish, how they currently are motivated to do things, and what they would like to change.
- Suggest solutions with clearly defined and agreed-on consequences as well as rewards that relate specifically to their goals.
- Get to the point.
- Provide options and let them make the decisions when possible.
- Let them know that you do not intend to waste their time.

How to Sell Your Product or Service to Socializers

With Socializers, be an especially empathic listener. Give positive feedback to let them know that you understand and can relate to what they are feeling. When you talk about yourself, remember to use feeling words instead of thinking words. To paraphrase this concept, share your vision of the world in terms of your emotions, opinions, and intuitions. Tell stories about yourself, especially humorous or unusual ones, to win the hearts (and sales) of

Socializers. Allow them to feel comfortable by also listening to their stories, even to the point of talking about topics that may stray from the subject.

Step #1: Making Contact With Socializers

When you write to or meet Socializers, give the letter or meeting an upbeat, friendly feeling and faster pace. The first time you call on Socializers, use a more open-ended, friendly approach. Tell them who you are and say something like, "I'd like to come by and show you an exciting new product that will analyze and organize your accounts and help you become even more of a top-performing salesperson."

When you meet Socializers, think (or more specifically, feel) in terms of someone running for election. Shake hands firmly, introduce yourself with confidence, and immediately show interest in them personally. Let them set the pace and direction of the conversation. Plan to have as many meetings with Socializers as necessary to build the relationship and gather information. After your first visit, you may want to meet for breakfast or lunch, because they are easier meals than dinner to put time limits on.

Step #2: Exploring Socializers' Needs

Socializers get bored quickly when they are not talking, so structure much of your information-gathering needs to revolve around them. But remember to strike a balance between listening to their stories and gathering the information you need to be an effective sales representative. When asking business questions, keep them brief. If you can, work these exploratory questions in with the social questions. "You mentioned people as one of the keys to your success. How do you find (recruit) the people you work with? What kind of training do you give them.?" The better your relationships with Socializers, the more willing they will be to cooperate and talk about the task at hand.

Socializers can be so open that they may tell you their fondest hopes and aspirations. If you can demonstrate how your product or service can get them closer to their dreams, they may become so excited about it—and you— that they are likely to sell themselves to you.

Step #3: Proposing Solutions for Socializers

Style is as important as substance, so be sure to sell the sizzle as well as the steak. Your presentation should show Socializers how your product or service will increase their prestige, image, or recognition. Talk about the favorable impact or consequences your suggestions will have in making their working relationships more enjoyable. Presentations need impact for people of this type, so involve as many of their senses as possible. Socializers want both the presentation and the product to feel great. Show them how you can save them effort and still make them look good. Back up your claims with testimonials from well-known people or corporations. Socializers respond well to the positive experiences that other people have had with your product or service, so tell them who else uses it. If one of their heroes tries something, they are likely to try it as well. Better yet, name some satisfied acquaintances that the Socializers know and admire. They may even respond with, "Go no further. If it's good enough for Pat Mullins, it's good enough for me. Pat probably spent weeks researching, comparing, and contrasting. That's the person you need on your payroll."

Step #4: Gaining Commitment With Socializers

Be open and ask, "Where do we go from here?" or, "What's our next step?" If your inventory is low, tell them. "I see you really are excited about this. I only have three left. Do you want one now?" Socializers are very spontaneous and respond well to the bandwagon approach of "everybody's doing it." If they like something, they buy it (all other things being equal). You may have to hold them back because they also tend to overbuy, a behavior that both you and your customer may live to regret. Although a handshake is usually good enough for them, you would be wise to have a written understanding. Both of you may hear the same words, but Socializers tend to interpret those words to their own advantage. For this reason, it may help to draw up a summary in advance and go over it with people of this type. Make absolutely sure that you agree on the specifics or, later on, you can almost guarantee on some degree of misunderstanding and disappointment.

Next, if required, change whatever details need changing and the job will be done, quickly and painlessly. Finally, go ahead and write up this agreement as a means of verification and send or, better yet, give them copies in person. Then you will have a much better chance at long-standing, productive business relationships.

Step #5: Assuring Socializers' Satisfaction

In business, Socializers frequently buy before they are sold. When they jump in too quickly, the probability that they may suffer buyers' remorse is higher than for those with other behavioral types. Socializers need ongoing reminders that they have made the right purchase decisions because they get bored quickly, even with new things. So make sure you reinforce their decisions by giving them plenty of service and/or assistance immediately after the sale. Be certain they actually do use your product; people of this type may get frustrated from incorrect usage and either put the product away never to be used again or return it for a refund. As a bonus for the extra effort, remember that they tend to talk up or talk down whatever comes into their minds. Because they mingle with so many people, you can even ask them if they would be willing to share with others their glowing testimonials about you and your product or service.

Sales and Service Strategies for Dealing With Socializers

- Show that you are interested in them, let them talk, and allow your animation and enthusiasm to emerge.
- Take the initiative by introducing yourself in a friendly and informal manner and be open to new topics that seem to interest them.
- Support their dreams and goals.
- Illustrate your ideas with stories and emotional descriptions that they can relate to their own goals or interests.
- Summarize clearly all of the details, directing them toward mutually agreeable objectives and action steps.
- Provide incentives to encourage quicker decisions.
- Give them testimonials.

How to Sell Your Product or Service to Relaters

Relaters want to maintain stability, so they want to know step-by-step procedures that meet their need for details and logical follow-through action. Organize your presentation—list specifics, show sequences, and provide data. If possible, outline your proposals or materials. Satisfy their need to know the facts, but also elicit their personal feelings and emotions by asking for their input on the "how-to" aspects.

Listen patiently to Relaters, projecting your true interest in them as individuals. Express your appreciation for their steadiness, dependability, and cooperative teamwork. Get to know Relaters personally; be nonthreatening, pleasant, friendly, but still professional. Develop trust, credibility, and friendship at a relatively slow, informal pace. Then communicate with Relaters consistently and regularly.

Step #1: Making Contact With Relaters

The best contacts with Relaters are soft, pleasant, and specific. Include the human element as well as references to things. Mention the name of the person who referred you. Remember, you may have the best product or service in the world, but if Relaters do not like you, they will settle for second best—or even fourth best—from a salesperson they like.

Step #2: Exploring Relaters' Needs

Relaters can be excellent interviewees. Talk warmly and informally and ask gentle, open questions that draw them out, especially around more sensitive areas. Show tact and sincerity in probing about their needs.

If they do not have good feelings about your product, company, or even you, they will not take the chance of hurting your feelings by telling you so. They want to avoid confrontations, even minor ones. Therefore, Relaters may tell you what they think you want to hear rather than what they really think. This same reticence may apply to telling you about their dissatisfaction with your competitors. Even though this is exactly what you want to hear, Relaters may avoid saying anything negative.

Step #3: Proposing Solutions for Relaters

Show how your product/service will stabilize, simplify, or support their procedures and relationships. Clearly define their roles and goals in your suggestions; include specific expectations of them in your plan. Present new ideas or variations from their current routines in a nonthreatening way. Provide them with the time and opportunities to adjust to changes in operating procedures and relationships. When change becomes necessary, tell them why. Explain how long the changes will take and any interim adjustments to current conditions. Design your message to impart a sense of stability, security, harmony, steadiness, and concrete benefits. Answer their concerns about how and what as well as you can. Reassure them that you will find out about the information they want to know; then do it. Stress that you are not initiating big changes, just helping them do better what they already do well.

Step #4: Gaining Commitment With Relaters

Relaters are slow, deductive decision makers. They listen to the opinions of others before making up their minds. So make a specific action plan. Provide personal guidance, direction, or assurance as required for pursuing the safest, most logical course to follow. When you reach agreement, try to explore any potential areas of misunderstanding or dissatisfaction. Relaters like guarantees that any new actions will involve a minimum level of risk, so offer assurances of support.

Try not to rush them, but do provide gentle, helpful nudges when needed to help them decide. Otherwise, they may postpone their decisions. Involve them by personalizing the plan and showing how it will directly impact them and their coworkers. Once you have determined which action is in their best interest, lead them to the confirmation with your recommendation. When you have reached agreement, you can gently lead Relaters to the next step.

Step #5: Assuring Relaters' Satisfaction

Practice consistent and predictable follow-up. Give them your personal guarantee that you will remain in touch, keep things running smoothly, and be available on an as-needed basis. Relaters like to think they have a special relationship with you, that you are more than just another business acquaintance. Remember that they dislike one-time deals, so follow up to maintain your relationship. Of all the types, Relaters most prefer a continuing, predictable relationship. Impersonal, computerized follow-through is not as appealing to people of this type, so continue building your business relationship with low-keyed attention and offers of assistance.

Sales and Service Strategies for Dealing With Relaters

- Get to know them personally.
- Approach them in a nonthreatening, pleasant, and friendly but professional way.
- Develop trust, friendship, and credibility at a relatively slow pace.
- Ask them to identify their own emotional needs as well as their task or business expectations.
- Get them involved by focusing on the human element; that is, how something affects them and their relationships with others.
- Avoid rushing them and give them personal, concrete assurances, when appropriate.
- Communicate with them in a consistent manner on a regular basis.

How to Sell Your Product or Service to Thinkers

Thinkers are efficiency experts who want to do their jobs as they want to do nearly everything else: the correct way. They also seek confirmation that they are right, but they typically will not ask. Thinkers go about tasks slowly so they have enough time to check things out; they dislike rushing or being rushed. Because Thinkers operate on a level that prefers thinking words rather than feeling words, build your credibility by remembering to think with your head, not with your emotions. Focus on their level of understanding about the what's and why's of your proposal.

Step #1: *Making Contact With Thinkers*

Before meeting, tell them briefly what you will cover so they know what to expect. This can be done when you make the appointment. Show them logical proof from reliable sources that accurately documents your quality, track record, and value. Once you have verified your credentials, preferably in writing or with tangible examples, you can establish credentials for your product or service as well. Speak slowly, and economize on words. Explain why you are contacting them. People of this type do not care much about social interaction (beyond courtesy and pleasantness), so get to the point. Avoid making small talk and speaking about yourself, except initially to establish your credibility. Thinkers tend to be somewhat humble and are naturally suspicious of those who flaunt themselves.

Step #2: *Exploring Thinkers' Needs*

Thinkers often like to answer questions that reveal their expertise, so they can be very good interviewees. As long as you ask logical, fact-oriented, relevant questions, they tend to enjoy talking to you. Phrase your questions to help them give you the right information. Ask open and closed questions that investigate their knowledge, systems, objectives, and objections. Let them show you how much they know, and make your own answers short and crisp. If you do not know the answer to something, don't fake it. Tell them you will find the answer for them by a certain time, and then do it.

Step #3: Proposing Solutions for Thinkers

Emphasize logic, accuracy, value, quality, and reliability. Present obvious disadvantages. Make your points, then ask Thinkers if they want further clarification. They dislike talk that is not backed up with both supporting evidence and action. Describe the process that you plan to follow, then outline how that process will produce the results they seek. Elicit specific feedback. People of this type are most likely to see drawbacks, so point out the obvious negatives before they do. Such honesty will only enhance your credibility. If you yourself do not draw attention to the disadvantages, Thinkers may view this as a cover-up. Instead, let them assess relative costs versus benefits, typical trade-offs when making realistic choices between competing products or services.

Step #4: Gaining Commitment With Thinkers

Provide logical options with documentation. Give them enough time and data to analyze their options. Unlike Directors and Socializers, people of this type are uncomfortable with snap decisions. When they say they will think about something, they probably are serious.

Unless Thinkers have already researched the field and determined that your product is the best, they probably will have your competitors call on them. Know your competition so that you can point out your advantages relative to what they offer. People of this type are likely to do their own comparative shopping, so mention your company's strengths as you suggest questions they may want to ask your competitors. In short, point out the things your company does as well or better than your competition. Do this in a factual, professional way that is based on allowing Thinkers to do a comparative cost-benefit analysis of the options.

Step #5: Assuring Thinkers' Satisfaction

Set a specific timetable for when you plan to measure success. Continue proving your reliability, quality, and value. Make yourself available for follow-up on customer satisfaction.

Sales and Service Strategies for Dealing With Thinkers

- Prepare, so that you can answer as many of their questions as soon as possible.
- Greet them cordially, but proceed quickly to the task; avoid starting with personal or social talk.
- Ask questions that reveal a clear direction and that fit into the overall scheme of things.
- Document how and why something applies.
- Give them time to think; avoid pushing them into hasty decisions.
- Tell them both the pros and cons and the complete story.
- Follow through and deliver what you promise.

10

Wrapping
It All Up

What Have You Learned?

You have come a long way since you began reading this book. You have learned more about others and about how others see you. You have learned specific strategies for dealing successfully with all kinds of people, even the most difficult. You have learned how to handle someone who is dominating and strongly opinionated. You have learned how to read someone's behavioral type over the phone, or through a letter, and how to prepare for a meeting or encounter with each of these types of people.

These strategies can benefit you in many ways—in better business relationships and hence, better business. They will help you to deal with the unpleasant but inevitable friction we all encounter at one time or another. You will be able to minimize annoying behaviors in others and recognize and reduce these same behaviors in yourself.

We would be delighted if, after reading this book, you went out and started practicing these new relationship techniques. This will not only help you become a better you, it will help you behave more maturely and productively by teaching you how to focus on your goals instead of your fears. Then you can develop and use more of your natural strengths, while recognizing, improving on, and modifying your weaknesses. It will not be easy and will require more practice, as well as some mistakes, to lead to greater success in communicating with others.

Do you remember when you first took on the challenge of learning how to drive a car? Before you learned how to drive, you were what we call an "unconscious incompetent." That is, you didn't know how to drive the car, and you didn't even know why you didn't know how to drive it.

When you first went out to learn how actually to drive the car, you became a "conscious incompetent": You still could not drive the car; but because of your new awareness of the automobile and its parts, you were consciously aware of why you couldn't drive it. From this step, you at least had the awareness of what you had to do to acquire the competency to drive.

With some additional practice and guidance, you were able to become competent in driving the car. However, you had to be consciously aware of what you were doing with all the mechanical aspects of the car as well as with your body. You had to be consciously aware to turn on your blinker signals well before you executed a turn. You had to remember to monitor the traffic behind you in your rear view mirror. You kept both hands on the wheel and monitored your car's position relative to the center-line road divider. You were consciously aware of all these things as you became a "consciously competent" driver.

Think of the last time you drove a car. Were you consciously aware of all the things we just discussed? Of course not! Most of us, after having driven for a while, progress to a level of "unconscious competency." This is the level where we can do something well and not even have to think about it. It comes naturally. It's habit.

The foregoing example holds true for relating effectively with others. You need to go through the competency processes to get to the highest level—the unconscious competence level. This is where you can communicate naturally and effectively. However, you have to pay a price to get to the level of unconscious competence: Practice, practice, practice.

When you were learning to drive the car, you acquired your competency through practice. For some of you, effectively relating with others may require a significant change of behavior. After persistence and practice, as you approach the unconscious competency level, your interpersonal relationship skills will increase beyond their previous level to a new and higher plateau.

If you have decided to accept the challenge of more effectively relating with others, the payoffs are certainly well worth your efforts. With so much to learn about, you are probably confused as to where to start.

We encourage you to get started this minute, before you do anything else. First, think about the goals you want to accomplish in the next year...the next month...the next week...and, finally, by the end of today! Develop a plan to meet those goals using the principles from this book.

Accept the Challenge

This first step requires your personal *commitment* to this challenge and *belief* in these principles. Their success is a proven fact and you can learn to put them to work for you. Of course, any skill takes practice, and you cannot realistically expect to put all of them into effect immediately. But, the minute you start to treat people they way *they* want to be treated, you will start to see progressive results. We encourage you to accept this opportunity to strengthen your relationship competencies!

Make a Plan

Once you have accepted the challenge, you need a plan to incorporate these techniques into your life. We have given you an extremely simple, effective method of identifying behavior styles, but one that takes some practice. Use these two questions:

- Is the person more Direct or more Indirect?

- Is the person more Self-Contained or more Open?

Practice by identifying the basic styles among members of your family, friends and coworkers. You may want to find a partner who wants to use these techniques also. Together you can discuss styles and help build your confidence in, and your proficiency with, these life skills.

Once you feel comfortable identifying the behavior styles of others, it is time to look at developing more adaptability in your own style. Think about one of your coworkers with whom you would like to improve your rapport. What kinds of tensions exist between you: Pace? Priority? How do you think you could reduce the tension to bring your coworker into his or her "comfort zone?" Develop an adaptability action strategy to use with that coworker. How will you know when you have developed better rapport with this person?

Whenever you feel the need, review the sections on Directors, Socializers, Relaters, and Thinkers. That will help you to identify whether people want a Direct or Indirect approach from you and whether they want you to be Self-Contained or Open in your dealings with them.

But, remember, there really is nothing mysterious about these techniques. You are just trying to treat people the way *they* want to be treated. If you are in doubt about a person's priorities (task or relationship), say something like, "I don't want to waste your time, but I would like to know you and your needs better. Do you prefer to spend some time getting to know the people you deal with? Or, do you prefer to get right down to the task at hand?" If you are watching body language, observing the environment, and listening, you probably won't have to ask those questions, but when in doubt, ask.

Be sure to make your plan include SMART goals (**S**pecific, **M**easurable, **A**chievable, **R**ealistic, and **T**rackable). When you see these techniques helping you achieve those goals, you will naturally be more motivated to continue to develop your ability to use them.

As you integrate our approach into your work style, you may find that it feels awkward at first, because it is different from the way you have been dealing with others. As you keep practicing, you will soon begin to notice that the new way is more comfortable than the old way for you. Before long, you will find that our approach will seem natural to you and you will begin to forget the way you used to deal with others.

Correctly used, these behavioral-style skills will allow you to interact with others, as well as solve problems in an open, honest atmosphere of trust and helpfulness. You will gain more support from others. You will deservedly feel an increased pride in your new and successful relationship strategies.

You need not wait; you can start to apply these skills immediately. The path has been mapped. Where you go from here depends on your determination and persistence in applying these skills.

Index